EATING THE LANDSCAPE

Eating the Landscape

American Indian Stories of Food, Identity, and Resilience

ENRIQUE SALMÓN

FIRST PEOPLES

New Directions in Indigenous Studies

THE UNIVERSITY OF
ARIZONA PRESS

TUCSON

The University of Arizona Press
www.uapress.arizona.edu

Printed in the United States of America

ISBN-13: 978-0-8165-3011-3 (paper)

Cover photo © Xavier Mascareñas/*The Daily Times*; Farmington, New Mexico. A Navajo bean crop manager holds pinto beans fresh from the fields.

Cover design by Leigh McDonald

Publication of this book was made possible, in part, with a grant from the Andrew W. Mellon Foundation.

Library of Congress Cataloging-in-Publication Data
Salmón, Enrique, 1958–
    Eating the landscape : American Indian stories of food, identity, and resilience / Enrique Salmón.
        p. cm. — (First peoples : New directions in indigenous studies)
    Includes bibliographical references and index.
    ISBN 978-0-8165-3011-3 (pbk. : alk. paper) 1. Indians of North America—Food—Southwest, New. 2. Indians of North America—Agriculture—Southwest, New. 3. Indians of North America—Southwest, New—Ethnic identity. I. Title.
    E78.S7S24 2012
    979.004'97—dc23

                                                          2011035703

♾ This paper meets the requirements of ANSI/NISO Z39.48-1992 (Permanence of Paper).

For Lisa

Contents

Figures

EATING THE LANDSCAPE

1

In My Grandmother's Kitchen

GRANDMA. THE DARK creases on my grandma's face deepened when she smiled. To my young mind, she seemed the perfect grandma. Her white hair contrasted with her dark brown skin. The brightness of the sun deepened the wrinkles and creases on her face. She cooked the best cactus fruit jam from the large prickly pears that grew behind the house. She always had cookies at hand when I came to visit. And she seemed to know everything about the land and food.

One day, in our yard, which was dotted with herbs and fruit trees, I watched her bend over to pick a sprig of *bawena* (spearmint) and hold it out for me to smell. Her old, faded cotton dress with the flower print outlined her frail 80-year-old frame. Her full set of teeth glistened as she smiled, watching me enjoy the scent. Then, in a voice made scratchy from smoking, she explained, "That is what *bawena* does to your stomach; it makes it smile." I cannot forget the many times when my grandma or my mother rescued my upset stomach with some hot tea of *bawena*. Always, after just one cup, my insides would begin to smile again, ready for some more food that I probably shouldn't have eaten.

I understand now what my grandma, my mother, as well as my grandfather and other family members were teaching me. They introduced me to Rarámuri traditional knowledge. I learned the names of plants, their uses, and their place in Rarámuri culture,

Figure 1.1 Chilis, chili powder, and chiltepines in a Rarámuri collection basket.

philosophy, and cosmology. I understood them to be relatives and living beings with emotions and lives of their own. I learned that they were part of my life as well and that I should always care for them. In short, my family led me into the traditional ecological knowledge of the Rarámuri.

My grandparents' souls now rest in the Milky Way with the other Rarámuri spirits that have departed this Earth. But their lessons live on in my memory. I recall my grandma's smiling face and her short, shuffling gait. If I am ill and drinking a steaming mug of *bawena*, I hear her scratchy voice describing the uses of other plants from our yard.

The knowledge I learned from my family was one aspect of a trove of culturally accumulated ecological knowledge. When they introduced me to individual plants, they also introduced my kinship to the plants and to the land from where they and we had emerged. They were introducing me to my relatives. Through this way of knowing, especially with regard to kinship, I realized a comfort and a sense of security that I was bound to everything around me in a reciprocal relationship.

The richest memories of my family are associated with plants. I frequently remember the seasonings my grandmother, mother, and aunts lovingly added to our meals. Epazote, cilantro, salvia, *yerba buena*, and, of course, *chili pequin* embodied the mural of flavors expressed at the table. These foods not only were eaten at home but also were central figures at fiestas, weddings, and other gatherings. I recall the many plant-related lessons I learned in my grandma's herb house. This latticed structure was filled with hanging dried and living plants as well as pungent and savory smells from the many herbs hanging from the ceiling. The roof was no longer visible through the layers of vines that draped over its eaves to the ground. On hot days, the interior would be nearly 10 degrees cooler. Inside, I would sit and watch my grandma grinding chilis and herbs in old stone metates and mortars while she talked about our origins and about our plant relatives. On my frequent visits there, I would enjoy the many aromas. It was during these times that she told me about the lives of plants and their characteristics. She described the relationships the plants had with each other. She taught me that the plants were not only plants but also people. Some were Rarámuri, whereas others were Apaches and non-Indians.

When I was older, my grandfather introduced me to plants while we shooed away crows and other critters from his corn, beans, and chilis[1] that grew in the large backyard garden he maintained in Chula Vista, California. Sometimes, I would help him rid the field of weeds using an old rusted hoe. The handle was gray with age, as the years of its being worked in the sun had faded the natural color of the wood. There was a fracture in the handle that had been repaired with pieces of old stained cotton material. There was no telling how old the tool was. I never asked my grandfather, as he rarely spoke, except to give orders and motion with his dark-skinned arm where I should be working. We would sit in the shade of a large fig tree for breaks. During these lapses in the work, I learned how corn and chili were our parents and protectors. He told me about the beginning of the world as he whittled on a piece of wood he had picked up somewhere. He taught me to respect the trees as relatives when he caught my cousins and me swinging from the rubbery limbs of his huge fig tree. From many of my immediate relatives, I gained scores of plant knowledge. It is difficult now to brew a cup of some medicinal herb for myself or for my children without picturing the specific time someone in my family introduced me to that particular remedy.

In most cases, I consumed the remedies as a result of something I should not have eaten. My cousins and I were budding herbalists. They were also my best friends. We roamed our communities in constant search of something to eat. We sucked on a succulent grass with yellow flowers we called lemon grass. Its juices resembled the tartness of real lemons. We found bushes full of red, juicy, and semisweet berries and filled ourselves to capacity with them. These and other plant foods became our emergency stores for the short treks that we imagined were epic adventures. Eventually, we encountered a plant we should not have eaten. Fortunately for us, we were related to wonderful and forgiving herbalists who could come to our stomachs' rescue.

Food was an essential ingredient at all our family gatherings. It blended with music, teasing, laughter, stories, and dancing to create a delicious, pungent celebration. Our celebrations were sometimes planned, but more often, impromptu events spurred by a cousin getting a new job, Dad getting a raise, or a family member having just returned from being gone for a length of time. Once it was decided that a celebration was in order, someone would soon ask, "What are we going to eat?"

Sometimes, the food itself would be cause for celebration. Every now and then, my Aunt Nick would bring over a bag of freshly picked avocados. To this day, I don't know where they came from or how she came to get the avocados, but she would just show up with a plain paper bag containing about 20 avocados ready to transform into guacamole or to simply slice and eat with salt, pepper, and salsa. Aunt Nick never knocked when she came into our little home. She would just enter and, setting the bag of avocados on the nearest flat surface, gruffly greet my mom or me. It was assumed by all that the fruits would be made into something to eat on the spot. Magically, and within 20 minutes, a feast was set before us, and we were eating. It was a requirement that there always be something to eat at our home, even if it was tortillas and beans.

Our family gatherings were and are loving and soulful times. Food, especially foods made by the hands of the people present, added to the soulful and loving feelings inherent in the space. Every day our food included tortillas, beans, and some kind of burrito or taco. We did not know that fajitas would someday become haute cuisine. My mom's tortillas were always near perfect circles. They were soft and pliable, and smelled best when returning home from a long day of being outside with my cousins. I could smell the aroma while still outside, letting my bicycle crash to the ground. Entering the house, I would inhale deeply in order to gloriously embrace the warmth of corn and flour masa being heated, pinto beans steaming on the stove, and a flimsy pile of newly cooked tortillas on the table behind where my mom stood by the oven. I enjoyed the fresh tortillas most with melted butter rolled up inside the hot circle. They also tasted great with a simple bowl of pinto beans swimming in the juices ladled into the bowl from the pot.

Cooking pinto beans was both a simple and a complex affair. I never ate canned beans until after I had left home, and they were unsatisfactory. Pinto beans, prepared from scratch, required only the hard, uncooked beans. They were always spread out on a table and sifted through for stones, dirt clods, and those wrinkled beans that appeared as though they had shriveled up in the sun. Then, they were prepared with pig's feet or salt pork, lard, epazote, and other secret spices. A pot of beans was more like a stew than a staple dish.

Foods that require an extra process before preparation such as beans, corn, and whole grains provide both a brush of texture and color to meal preparation and further community involvement in their process from harvest to meal. When helping my mom sort the hidden stones from the beans, I used to place a single shiny bean inside my mouth and flick it with my tongue in order to bounce it against the insides of my teeth. I sometimes wondered whether a plant would begin to sprout inside my body if I did that long enough or if I accidentally swallowed the bean. My mom used to warn me that the beans were dirty and worried that I would get sick. I figured that I had swallowed so many germs already in my daily activities as a kid that one semidirty bean wouldn't cause any more harm. I knew where the beans had come from. In some cases,

I had helped collect beans from their semidried and dried encasements hanging from their stalks. This kind of tactile knowledge contributed to my overall library of food-related knowledge. Strangely, I would not be able to identify the source of most of my food understanding from my childhood. I just simply knew it. It has become part of the volumes of the library of traditional knowledge encoded in the language of my family experiences and added to during later interactions with land-based indigenous people.

Of course, we ate our family version of tacos, tostadas, burritos, and other northern Mexican cuisine; but it would be difficult to compare our version of these dishes to those in a typical Mexican restaurant. This is because the preparation and ingredients associated with these foods reflected our unique collective family history and experiences, especially those connected to landscapes.

When the occasion was more than impromptu, the king and queen of celebration foods emerged: carne asada and tamales. Carne asada—beef strips marinated in various blends of spices, citrus juices, and herbs—would cause my first cousin's mouth to water at its very mention. Beer was an essential accompaniment with carne asada. We would drive miles out of our way to find the very best carne asada either preprepared and brought home in plastic bags while still marinating, or cooked and speedily couriered by a relative to the party location. It was best cooked outside over a barbeque and eaten with tortillas. Tamales arrived on a plate in front of the eater in a variety of incarnations, depending on which member of the family had supervised the preparation. One could identify the maker by the signature ingredients, softness of the corn masa, and amount of filling. One never dared mention a preference of tamales in public for fear of some kind of familial retribution. Besides, they were all good, and recipes were often amalgams of several current and past family members' recipes. Still, there was this underlying competition surrounding tamales that was pursued by the tamale chefs in the family. In our case, it included most of the married women. Although they all preached the beauty and love associated with the fact that the important thing was that we all had enough to eat, I recall watching my various aunts eyeing us as we ate their tamales. They paid attention to the ephemeral qualities of the gusto we poured into our tamale eating. They secretly counted how many of their, or their sisters' tamales we ate and noted whether we made comments or other such eating-related noises. I never told anyone, especially my mom, but I really enjoyed most the tamales made by her best friend, Eloisa. She was not a blood relative and became a friend of my mom's when I was very young after having moved into Eloisa's neighborhood. Eloisa's tamales were always moist and could be counted on to contain a hefty spicy pork filling offset by the unusual inclusion of raisins. The raisins were unique and special. I can still recall the first time I bit into her tamales. At first, my mouth was surprised at the squirt of raisin juice among the familiar spices and textures. Quickly, I realized the ingredient and have searched for this kind of tamale ever since.

Tamale-making parties always preceded the actual celebration. The female members of the family would gather, drink margaritas, laugh, make sordid remarks about the men in the family, and simply have fun. By the end of the tamale-making fiesta, the laughter was loud and raucous. I enjoyed watching my mother during these times as she opened up and became more loving than her normal self, which was especially loving to begin with. At celebrations where tamales were served, we searched for the tamales that were made at the end of the tamale-making party. We could distinguish them by their fatness.

Recipes were shared during celebrations and whenever family came together. They are a form of knowledge reproduction and social exchange. They gave everyone something to talk and gossip about, to share, and to be proud of. Without the sharing of recipes, the family community begins to dissolve. The tamale-making parties have vanished from our family. No one has time to spend preparing the masa and to get together. Anniversaries and weddings have to be planned a year in advance. Invitations are sent out as far in advance of the celebration as possible in order for family members to make time in their calendars. Today, in many neighborhoods where there is a large Hispanic community nearby, couples walk the street holding between them a large pressure cooker or ice chest filled with hot tamales. They arrive at the front doors of strangers' homes selling the contents of their burden in order to make ends meet. What was once a celebration food has become a source of supplementary income.

I have eaten my share of tamales, but I have no idea who made them and under what circumstances. Perhaps laughter accompanied the making; I would hope so. Nevertheless, these tamales do not connect me to a community. My identity and culture as a Mexican is reaffirmed whenever I eat tamales, but not the unique community with whom I grew up and from where my understanding of my identity and its connection to a landscape emerged. My reaffirmation of identity and connection to place is not a direct result of the tamales, but comes more from the processes that surround tamales, beans, raisins inside of tamales, and my grandmother's herbal teas. The processes interconnect family, landscape, collection knowledge, story, and an encoded library of cultural and ecological knowledge, all of which sustain and revitalize a sense of self and place. A statistic I read on a back of a milk carton one morning revealed that people who ate so many meals with their families suffered less from crimes and other social ills. This milk-carton morality reflects, I feel, the consequences of modern society that is removed from a direct relationship to its food and from the social process related to eating any landscape.

Eating a landscape is more than the act of eating. Vandana Shiva suggests that eating is a political act. Through our choices to eat locally or to eat food that has traveled 2,000 miles to reach our grocer's shelves, we support a process. The latter process consumes precious fossil fuels; wastes clean drinking water in order to raise animal products; knocks down fragile rain forests and desert landscapes; and increases nutrition-related diseases primarily among poor, low-income, and uneducated populations. Eating a landscape is also a socially reaffirming act. In the case of my family, whenever I partake of Eloisa's tamale recipe or my mother's way of preparing salsa, I am eating the memories and knowledge associated with those foods. The elements of the stories, the jokes, and the intricate contextualized experience become embodied every time the eating takes place. It becomes a form of mimetic regeneration to eat one's family's recipes.

Eating is not only a political act but also a cultural act that reaffirms one's identity and worldview each time one sits down to a plate of home-cooked beans or *sopa de albondigas*. Culture is performed by humans every minute of every day. Eating our culture and our familial memories is another ritual that is performed throughout our lives. How we remember our lines for this ongoing stage act happens each time we prepare to do something cultural, such as eating old family recipes. In other words, we often eat our family, our culture. Leslie Marmon Silko reminds us in *Yellow Woman and a Beauty of the Spirit* that we "depend upon the collective memory through successive generations to maintain and transmit an entire culture, a worldview complete with proven strategies for survival." We have to eat in order to survive; therefore, food becomes a medium through which a complex of collective memories from generations of preparing tamales remains alive and intact.

As a result, because so much of the food we are discussing in this book comes directly from the land, food landscapes remain intact when old recipes are regenerated. The food itself, and the landscapes from which it emerges, remembers how it should be cooked. This can happen because the food itself activates in us an encoded memory that reminds us how to grow, collect, and prepare the food. The land and food then become the source of knowledge and history. Many recipes are dynamic, as they get altered and tailored to family changes, history, and events. Often a family member will change the recipe, or someone new to the family will cause this to happen. The specific family members may change, but the food and the land where it grows remain the source of the cultural memory. Some might suggest that this is inauthentic, incomplete, or not dependable knowledge; but in fact, this kind of collective memory is more accurate because it reflects the position of the family and culture at the moment. Each recipe addition is valuable as it adds to the continuous composition of the culture and family. What happens is that the recipes act like stories that are told and retold in different ways depending on the storyteller or, in this case, the cook. Because they are family recipes, they are also communal. Communal storytelling has a way of correcting itself. The corrections are not seeking absolute truth, but communal truth. An example is when Aunt Nick might remind Aunt Vera that that wasn't the spice that Grandma used in the salsa, and then Vera responds with a correction from a different experience and point in family history. These kinds of debates are not merely family disputes or arguments, but act as self-correcting landmarks and also as mediums through which critical family history is recounted and corrected.

In my family, we carried on a tradition dating back centuries when we grew much of our own food. My grandma always maintained her collection of special herbs while my grandfather grew his small fruit orchard, corn, and nopalitos, which were all important ingredients in many meals. Indigenous people around the world still subsist on much of what they can grow. Their practices and agricultural traditions maintain crucial legacies on the landscapes that they manage. Thousands of varieties of landraces and unique vegetables, fruits, legumes, and livestock depend on the farmers that continue to husband them. Many of these crops, such as corn, would revert to their prehuman state within a few years if it were not for human manipulations that maintain their present forms. These varieties of plants and animals remain our human legacy, our contribution to diversity so long as we maintain our relationship to the landscapes where we live.

An essential lesson for us, as we continue on our current self-destructive path of monocropping, genetically modifying our food using artificial irrigation, and overfertilizing, will be to relearn how to cook our landscapes: the manner in which we sustainably steward our food crops, relying on a process that began in our home kitchens. We also need to rely on our family collective memories around foods or begin to regenerate new and old ones where recipes begin on the landscapes from where the foods grew and where, hopefully, we had some kind of hand in growing them. This could be reflected in actually maintaining our own small farm or garden, visiting local farmer's markets or becoming members of community supported agriculture (CSA), or getting fresh foods from local small-scale traditional farmers. In fact, the premise of this book is that our current hope for a future of safe, tasty, and sustainable food rests in the knowledge of the small number of quickly disappearing small farmers and their farmlands.

Foods are only one of many concerns when we regard the future of humanity on this planet; but it is an essential one when we consider how we will adapt to global warming, which will include growing foods that can withstand droughts, higher temperatures, and other extreme climatic changes. The solutions, however, may be located in the tiny fields of O'odham Ak-Chin farmers, northern New Mexico bean growers, and Hopi kivas. O'odham corn and beans were hybridized by O'odham farmers centuries ago to withstand little moisture and intense heat. Practices such as these will be valuable lessons for the future of land and agricultural management. Temperature variation and low rainfall are only two issues traditional farmers used to and continue to deal with in their gamble to grow food. In the future, additional challenges for agriculture will be mutating pests, too much rain, loss of topsoil, loss of farmlands, and terminal seed created by the giant agricultural industry. Except for the latter, indigenous farmers maintain solutions for these issues.

This book will reveal a handful of small indigenous farmers in the American Southwest and in northwest Mexico. The narrative will explore how these dedicated stewards of foods continue to enhance the beauty of the places where they live and how what they continue to do may in fact hold the key to humanity's food and environmental future.

Note

1. I choose to use the Nahuatl-derived form of spelling *chili* (pronounced "she-lay"), as this is the form with which Mexican and Native eaters in the Greater Southwest are most familiar.

2

Sharing Breath

The Grass Is Not Always
Greener on the Other Side

IT WAS A WARM afternoon in the Sierra Madres of Chihuahua, Mexico. I was engaged there in some of my dissertation fieldwork as I visited the government classes at the boarding school in Nararáchi, a small mountain village of Rarámuri. The students arrived early Monday mornings from their scattered rancherías (small multifamily agricultural communities) and returned home on Friday afternoons. On this particular afternoon, the students were learning history, and the lesson focused on the Mexican Revolution. The young instructor, on a 6-month government assignment to teach in this rural area, was from Mexico City. The instructor spoke in Spanish while discussing the glories of Pancho Villa, Zapata, Carranza, and the despotism of Díaz. He neither mentioned Rarámuri involvement in the revolution, although many Rarámuri men were conscripted into the Mexican army during the revolution, nor discussed the effects of the revolution on Rarámuri families and individuals. Although I never heard her tell her experiences about the revolution, I was often reminded about the moments when my grandmother would retell how her family ranchito in Chihuahua was raided by Pancho Villa when she was a child. The government instructor was reciting the official Mexicanized version of history,

12

Figure 2.1 Rarámuri family walking to Norogachi, Chihuahua, Mexico.

which, unfortunately, reminded the students very little of who they were.

Cultural history and biocultural lessons are woven into the daily fabric of Rarámuri activities. Rarámuri stories are about how the world began, how the animals emerged, and how the first Rarámuri found their way to this level of the universe. Their history also explains how the plants are direct relatives to the people. For me, as an indigenous ethnobotanist, the stories serve as conduits through which I can express my culture's perceptions of how the natural world developed and why it acts the way it does. The stories also provide metaphors and cultural models from which I can interpret actions and interactions between the people and the plants. The stories are essential for understanding Rarámuri models of the natural world.

The Mexican Revolution suspended agriculture in some areas because supporters of Pancho Villa raided Rarámuri *rancherías* for food and sometimes young girls, whom they forced into servitude. My grandmother's story about Pancho Villa included a part about how her parents would hide her in the corncrib when the Villistas came looking for food. Often, the young Rarámuri men were "volunteered" into military service either by the Mexican army or by the revolutionaries. One reason that my Rarámuri grandfather first ended up in the United States was to escape serving in the military.

During the week away at school, the children are engulfed in an alien culture and education. They are indoctrinated into the Mexican way of perceiving history, which will influence their future perspectives of the land. After the Mexican Revolution, the land became something to dominate. Later, the Green Revolution of the 1960s launched the notion that the land and the people who worked it were there for the good of the continuing revolution. However, when the children go home to their own communities and traditions, their histories differ, along with their perceptions of the land.

The focus of Western cultural history is heroes. The people that influence events are usually the ones that dominate, lead, and conquer; they are normally the focus of history lessons. The focus of Rarámuri cultural history is instead the landscape. The heroes are the trees, plants, animals, and children. The land, plants, and people share the landscape rather than dominate it. The Rarámuri origin story offers an example of this understanding.

In the beginning, matter and *iwígara* (the breath of life) met. From this meeting, *Onorúame* (the Creator) was conceived and born. After he matured, *Onorúame* created the land. On the land, *Onorúame* placed many of the animals, including deer, rabbits, turkeys, owls, eagles, fish, bats, and the bear. He made insects fly in the air and crawl on the ground. At first, the land was flat and featureless. Therefore, *Onorúame* asked *Ohí*, the bear, to shape the land with his claws. The bear shaped the Sierra Tarahumara, other nearby mountains ranges, the arroyos, and the deep barrancas. Plants were created after the land was shaped. Many of these plants were considered humans by the Rarámuri, whereas others became plants after they first lived as humans.

The first Rarámuri were corrupt and lazy. They had been created by *Onorúame* and sent to the Earth, falling from the sky like raindrops. Their lives were short, so they ran everywhere in order to accomplish their daily tasks. But they did not appreciate the lives given to them by the Creator and gambled constantly, neglecting their fields, each other, and the land. Out of disgust, *Onorúame* organized a huge extended rainstorm, flooding the entire region and killing the people.

On a hilltop in the Sierra, two children, a boy and a girl, survived the flood. The children were scared at first, but *Onorúame* consoled them. The children then became lonely, missing all their friends and relatives. *Onorúame* assured them that they would not be lonely for long. He asked them to be patient and said he would find a way to alleviate their situation. On the third day of their isolation, *Onorúame* appeared before the children and gave them some corn seed. He instructed them to wait for the waters to recede, then to go about scattering the seeds. From the seeds, he said, new life would emerge. In three days, the waters began to dry up, and the children walked about scattering the seeds. As *Onorúame* had said, new life began to sprout.

At first, the corn plants grew as normal ones. Their stalks were strong. The leaves reached all the way down to the earth. Eventually, ears sprouted from the intersections of stalk and leaf, and corn silk appeared. But soon the process changed. One day, the children noticed human heads emerging from the ears. They could see the black hair on top of the heads, then the foreheads, and soon the entire heads and bodies sprung forth from the ears of corn and sprawled out onto the ground. This was happening everywhere the corn plants grew. In a short time, the land had been repopulated with Rarámuri. Those two children, who tossed the seeds around after the flood, are the reason that the Rarámuri live in small isolated communities. When they scattered the corn seeds, they also scattered the people. Today, many Rarámuri continue to think of themselves as the children of corn.

To most Rarámuri, the world outside the Sierra Tarahumara is uncertain and dangerous. Among the people, there are tales of giants from the north and east, and of *Chabochi*, the bearded ones

(nonindigenous people) from the south. The Rarámuri word for
north, *michu*, is similar to that of the Nahuatl god of death, *mict-
lanticutli*. The word for west, *tobuku*, also means to submerge.
This meaning suggests a Rarámuri explanation for what happens to
the sun each evening. *Ori* is the word for east. It means to return.
South is expressed with the word *tugeke*, which is very close to the
word *tuga*, meaning to roast. But *tu* is also an old Uto-Aztecan
word for south.

Most Rarámuri would prefer to remain within the mountains
and canyons that comprise *Gawi Wachi*, the place of nurturing. In
a very real way, the mountains and canyons have always protected
the people from disease and European encroachment. The stories
reflect the protective nature of the Sierra. In order to escape the
flood, the two children fled to the safety of a high place. People still
live in the numerous caves of the Sierra and canyons. Caves act also
as Rarámuri expressions of safety. A Rarámuri story recounts how
when the sun came too close to the earth, it burned everyone except those living in caves. Mountains, caves, and canyons are not
only symbols of safety but also expressions and symbols of rebirth.
Yet the symbols carry over to actions as well. Peyote ceremonies,
rituals of rebirth, and journeys to the other reality take place in
caves. The Rarámuri dead are buried in caves. Mountains remain
symbols of strength and of refuge.

The mountains of the Sierra Tarahumara support not only the
levels of the universe but also Rarámuri culture and cosmology.
They afford food a sense of place. This is because the mountains
and barrancas are directly connected to the creation of the world
and offer an unbroken continuity to the creation of the land, as
well as a kincentric connection to Rarámuri origins and the creation
of other living things such as plants.

The Rarámuri folk classification system includes gendered plants,
plants identified as *Chabochi*, plants who are indigenous, and plants
who are Rarámuri. The categories of plants are indistinguishable
from the Rarámuri categories of humans and, to a large extent, mir-
ror human social categories. In addition, the moral and behavioral
attributes of these human social categories are projected onto the
corresponding categories of plant people.

The Rarámuri are at the first level of a hierarchy. At the next level below, *Chabochi* are contrasted with indigenous people. At the next level, indigenous people are divided into Rarámuri and other indigenous people. These Rarámuri often separate themselves into *Cimarronis*, the wild ones, and Gentiles, those who converted to Catholicism. This category of other indigenous people, according to the Rarámuri, includes Apache, Yaqui, Opata, Guarijio, Tepehuán, and Mayo.

Sunú (corn) is female. Many of the terms associated with corn suggest that corn is mother's milk and breasts. The name also suggests mother's milk. *Wásia* (*Ligusticum porteri*) is a female as well. The word *wasi* also means mother-in-law. *Sitákame* (*Haematoxylon brasiletto*) is a female plant whose characteristics note special attention. A story from the eastern Sierra tells that *Sitákame* was at one time a human who quarreled with everyone. She got angry when she lost at gambling and started fights at *tesguinadas* (ritual corn-beer drinking gatherings). She quarreled with *wásia*, tobacco, and even squash. *Onorúame* eventually lost his patience with *Sitákame* and "changed her into a plant." But *Sitákame*'s female associations do not end there. *Sitákame*'s inner heart wood is red and is used for several remedies but especially for excessive bleeding during the menstrual period and after childbirth. In the story, *Sitákame* is afforded human characteristics, emotions, failings, and personality. She has a sister and acquaintances, but loses her human lifestyle due to a human addiction to gambling.

Male plants include pine trees, piñons and junipers, oaks, tobacco, beans, squash, peyote, and datura. All these plants, except *Sitákame*, were originally created in their plant form. In the minds of Rarámuri, they are not anthropomorphized. Instead, they are human but with different features. My grandfather used to mention how *Bawákawa* (Tobacco) and *Baka-bu bahi* (Corn Husk) used to drink corn beer together. In his husky voice, he imitated the voices of Tobacco and Corn Husk as they asked for the drinking gourd and told stories of other plants. Long ago, when plants could speak as do humans, plants talked with the Rarámuri, Tobacco and Corn Husk were drinking friends. They drank together at *tesguinadas* and gambled together. They had a mutual friend named Drinking

Gourd, who would meet them at *tesguinadas*. Together, they became beautifully drunk. This is why smoking is expected at *tesguinadas*. This story not only illustrates the human qualities applied to plants but also offers a cultural explanation for a particular tradition by applying what are expected to be proper human actions to plants.

But tobacco, smoke, and fire carry additional weight in Rarámuri ritual and prayer. The Rarámuri smoke only at night so as not to confuse the Creator, who might mistake the smoke for clouds. If this should happen, he might not produce real clouds for making rain. Smoke from tobacco and that from pine resin incense are employed as healing agents. Smoke is a visible aspect of breath that permeates all life. Blowing smoke into a patient is how some healers strengthen their patients' breath. In addition, fire is an element of every Rarámuri gathering, ceremony, dance, and ritual. *Semana Santa* (Holy Week) ceremonies do not begin until the first evening when fires are lit atop the mesas and high points surrounding the communities. Evil characters associated with *Diablo* are scared of fire and so will not visit the dance and ceremony.

Food plants and many other plants are female, because they take care of us and feed us. Female plants tend to be domesticated food plants or plants used for general healing or for female ailments. Male plants tend to be potentially dangerous, ceremonial, used by experienced healers, and are often not related to the Rarámuri.

A healer from the Sierra was telling me about *híkuli* (peyote) being a Rarámuri. I asked him how he knew that *híkuli* was a human. He said, "*Híkuli*, and other plants, talk to me. I hear them when I walk near them. Sometimes they talk to me in dreams." To the healer and to other Rarámuri, the plants exist at the same level as humans. They speak to us. Plants are also broken down into indigenous groups. Although some people consider *bakánawi* to be *Chabochi*, they are sometimes seen as Apache due to their fierceness and unpredictability. Some *híkuli* are Apache as well due to the unpredictability of the species.

It is not surprising that the Apache are singled out as related to dangerous plants. The Apache often raided stores of corn and animals, stole children and women, and killed our warriors. The animosity between the two peoples revealed itself when Rarámuri warriors volunteered to scout for the Mexican army during the 1880s when Apache raids were especially virulent. It is reported that a Rarámuri named Mauricio single-handedly killed the war chief Victorio in 1880.

Many important plants are Rarámuri. The category includes some hallucinogenic plants, but does not include plants that are fatally toxic. It is not surprising that the majority of these plants are useful and are often used in healing and other ceremonies. *Sunú* (corn) is a Rarámuri, as are the domesticated plants *muní* (beans), *bachi* (squash), and *korí* (chili). *Sitákame* is a Rarámuri. She is used for female bleeding problems, jaundice, weak blood, and weak hearts. The wood of this small tree is prized for making staffs of office for community leaders and is carved for the rasping sticks still used in ceremonies. The true peyote, *híkuli* (*Lophophora williamsii*), is not consumed by all Rarámuri. Some fear the plant, saying that it will make a person go crazy; nevertheless, many Rarámuri continue to consume *híkuli*.

A false peyote called *híkuli cimarroni* (*Ariocarpus fissuratus*) is also a Rarámuri, but is, as the borrowed Spanish name implies, one of the "wild ones." During the period of the Jesuits, many Rarámuri never converted to Catholicism because they either were rebellious or were situated so deep in the far reaches of the barrancas that they never encountered the missionaries. Many *cimarronis*, as they are called by other Rarámuri, still live in the far corners of the canyons and are said to still carry bows and arrows.

One warm afternoon, I was sipping *cokas* (Pepsi Colas) with some Rarámuri friends in the small one-room *Conasupo* (small government-sponsored general store and trading post) at the edge of Norogachi when in walked three traditionally dressed Rarámuri. I noticed they were leaner and darker than the Rarámuri living around Norogachi. Their dress was cut slightly different, and they wore leather-soled instead of car-tire sandals. I also noticed they carried water gourds and bows and arrows. When the newcomers entered, everyone quickly became quiet and cautiously stared at them. The three asked for *cokas*, which they quickly and quietly sipped. Their eyes darted around at the contents of the room and at us. We must have looked like the timid rabbits that they, no doubt, hunted with their bows. One of them traded some herbs for a col-

Figure 2.2 Rarámuri Yúmari ceremony, Nararáchi, Chihuahua, Mexico.

orful cloth. They finished their drinks and quickly left. No one spoke for a moment. Finally, a friend broke the silence and whispered, "*Cimarronis.*"

Although *bakánawi* (*Scirpus acutus, Coryphantha compacta, Ipomoea purpurea*) are considered by some Rarámuri to be *Chabochi*, others say this group of plants is Apache. But, for the most part, *bakánawi* are categorized as Rarámuri. The uncertain classification of *bakánawi* is most likely a result of the three species of plants that share the name. There are several uses of the *bakánawi*. The disproportionately large tuber of the species of *Ipomoea purpurea* is carefully collected and used to help people who are crazy or have lost parts of their soul.

Wásia (*Ligusticum porteri*) is a plant that possesses both medicinal and magical qualities. *Wásia* has always been a Rarámuri; she just looks like a plant. It is one of *Onorúame*'s favorite beings, but is hated by *Diablo* and sorcerers. Many Rarámuri carry a piece of *wásia*'s hairy root around their neck or in a small pouch in their waist sash. It is said to repel the evils and spells of sorcerers, to bring good luck, and to ward off rattlesnakes. It is used in nearly every healing ceremony in the form of a tea, which is consumed to treat several ailments.

Kori (chili) was once a Rarámuri who was transformed into a plant by *Onorúame*. *Kori* was changed into a plant for fighting with two other Rarámuri plants: *Sitákame* and *habi-ki* (species undetermined). *Kori* is also attributed with the power to repel sorcery; one eats kori to scare away sorcerers. It is a part of nearly every meal throughout the Sierra Tarahumara and is used as a medicine for both people and animals.

Other plants that are Rarámuri include *okoko, Pinus* spp., *aorí, Juniperus deppeana, bisíkori, Pinus edulis, seréke, Dasylirion simplex, sokó, Yucca decipiens, ruyá, Nolina matapensis,* and *rohísawa, Quercus* spp. But plants make up only a small segment of the entire ecosystem of the Sierra Tarahumara, which is seen as tied directly to Rarámuri identity.

The Rarámuri are part of an extended ecological family that shares ancestry and origins. We share awareness that life in any environment is viable only when humans view the life surrounding them as kin. The kin, or relatives, include humans as well as all the natural elements of the ecosystem. We are affected by and, in turn, affect the life around us. The interactions that result from this "kincentric ecology" enhance and preserve social structure and the ecosystem. Interactions are the commerce of social and ecosystem functioning. Without human recognition of their role in the complexities of life in a place, the life suffers and loses its sustainability. I call this sphere of thought kincentricity because it encompasses several senses: the way in which plant names are learned, ecological roles of plants, and seeing plants as kin that are linked through *iwígara*.

One evening, I went to Cusarare to watch the *matachine* dances. I stood in the doorway at the old adobe church and watched the dancers, who were arranged in two lines, reel back and forth to the repetitive violin music. After several repetitions, the colorfully attired dancers whooped, then whirled, interlaced the dancing lines, and continued. Along the walls of the church, many Rarámuri stood or sat on the floor. They watched the ceremony in silence, although their eyes reflected their concentration on the dancers. Some tourists were there, including a group of Europeans.

After many whoops and whirls, the *chapeon*, or dance leader, signaled for the music to stop. The dancers left the church and went to a patio across the church square to drink suwi-ki. During the break, a tourist that had been watching the dancers approached me and asked why only a few Rarámuri were dancing. I said, "They are all dancing; some dance with their breath." At all Rarámuri dances, there will be nondancers sitting nearby, leaning against a church wall or a railing, standing with their arms crossed against the cold. They might have their blankets draped over one shoulder with stern faces and eyes intent on the events. These people are not spectators, but like supporters at a healing ceremony, offer their thoughts and energy toward the dancers as a way to strengthen the intentions of the ceremony. In this way, they boost the dancers' intention of keeping the land strong.

The Rarámuri believe that human breath is shared by all surrounding life and that our emergence into this world was possibly caused by some of the nearby life-forms. From this awareness, we understand that we are responsible for the survival of all life. As a result, we are cognizant of human kincentric relationships with nature similar to those shared with family and tribe. A reciprocal relationship has been fostered, with the realization that humans affect nature and nature affects humans. This awareness influences Rarámuri interactions with the environment. These interactions, or cultural practices of living with a place, are manifestations of kincentric ecology.

At *yúmari* ceremonies, dances and songs are performed to heal people as well as animals and the land. During such a ceremony, the women dance in a continual *iwí* (circle), while the male singers and chanters dance within the counterclockwise-moving circle. Circles are a central focus of Rarámuri worldview and life. Everything happens in circles; therefore, circles are honored, cherished, and ritualized. *Yúmari* dances are not the only events at which one will notice Rarámuri dancing or even moving in circles. *Matachine* dancers stand in lines, but individually they spin around in place. Pinto dancers during *Semana Santa* are constantly spinning, as are the singers and chanters accompanying the various dancers. The songs of these singers ask that the land be nourished and that the land nourish the people. As the songs are performed, the *iwí* continues to turn. The *iwí* represents the fertility of the land and also roughly translates into the idea of binding with a lasso. But it also means to unite, to join, and to connect. Another meaning of *iwí* is to breathe, inhale/exhale, or respire. The word *iwí* is used to identify a metamorphosing caterpillar that weaves its cocoons on the Madrone trees (*Arbutus* sp.) The implication is that a whole morphological process of change, death, birth, and rebirth is associated with circles.

Iwigá means soul, which can be an elusive concept, even among the Rarámuri, to whom it means different things depending on who is talking. It can mean not only life force but also breath. Generally, however, it is the soul, or *iwigá*, that sustains the body with the breath of life. Everything that breathes has a soul. Plants, animals, humans, stones, the land, all share the same breath.

When a Rarámuri child becomes sick, the parents offer food to a creek or pond in hopes that this will attract the child's lost soul back to the child. Rarámuri parents are often afraid to move a sick child to a hospital that is so far away from home because it will be difficult for the child's soul to find its way back to the child.

Iwígara is the soul or essence of life everywhere. Therefore, *iwígara* is the idea that all life—spiritual and physical—is interconnected in a continual cycle. We are all related to and play a role in the complexity of life. To the Rarámuri, the concept of *iwígara* encompasses many ideas and ways of thinking unique to the place in which the Rarámuri live. Rituals and ceremonies, the language, and, therefore, Rarámuri thought are influenced by the lands, animals, and winds with which they live. *Iwigá* reflects the total geomythic interconnectedness and integration of all life in the Sierra Madres.

The geomythic landscape of the Sierra Tarahumara becomes most clear with regard to managing the land. The use of plants for healing and for food becomes a window through which to see Rarámuri participation in the natural community. The origin stories and those of the plant relatives show how we are a part of the land onto which we were placed as stewards. We are also directly responsible for the health of the Creator, who works hard each day to provide for the land and its inhabitants.

In return for Rarámuri care, the land provides a cornucopia. *Sepé* (wild greens) are collected by nearly all Rarámuri to augment the daily diet of corn, beans, potatoes, squashes, wheat, and a variety of other products, both Old World and New World in origin. The land also permits the raising of goats, sheep, chickens, and pigs. Some Rarámuri raise cows and horses. Nondomesticated or wild plants are available from the land as well.

This rich area offers many wild plant medicines, most of which are utilized by the Rarámuri. The Rarámuri also utilize many natural materials from the forests and barrancas, including *basíkori* and piñon, for building and fuel. For household use and as a way to supplement their meager incomes, they weave baskets of sotol leaves, pine needles, and yucca leaves. Many baskets and other crafts are sold to the expanding tourist industry.

Most Rarámuri still collect edible greens that are dried and stored to be eaten later. They recognize and harvest many plants used for colds, arthritis, baskets, stomachaches, corn beer, bruises, the blood, and headaches. Collecting trips are neither special fractions of time nor specifically planned. Plants are collected as one walks to the *Conasupo* (trading post), as Rarámuri come over to visit, or during in between times when they enjoy stopping by the creek to toss rocks into the water.

The Sierra Tarahumara is a highly biodiverse region. The eight physiognomic vegetation types found in the region include montane evergreen and oak-coniferous woodlands, tropical deciduous forests, oak savannas, chaparral, short-grass prairie, subtropical thornscrub, and subtropical desert fringe. This area houses the third largest concentration of biodiversity in the world with 4,000 vascular plant species, 150 of which are endemic. In addition, over time the people have managed to hybridize 18 pre-Columbian food crops including agaves, pepperweed, panic grass, tepary beans, squashes, and several maize varieties. It is no accident that the area is so diverse; there is a strong link between cultural diversity and biodiversity. Indigenous land managers have ensured a sustainable lifestyle for several centuries.

North of the US–Mexico border, traditional diets have been in decline for several generations as an unfortunate result of Manifest Destiny. Many of today's young Native people in the United States are raised in a Big Gulp culture consisting primarily of fried processed foods, fast foods, and carbonated and sweetened drinks. These diets are low in fiber and high in fats and simple carbohydrates. In northwest Mexico, a Big Gulp type of diet has not yet taken hold. Kids are kids no matter where they eat. In the Sierra Tarahumara, the youngsters enjoy sugary drinks and candy, but fortunately for their pancreases, they have little access to nor can they afford to shop often at convenience stores and fast-food restaurants. This lack of ease to attain processed foods may be saving them. And although many indigenous peoples eat the mestizo diet, this diet remains relatively healthy, consisting of *tortillas de trigo* (white flour tortillas), which are preferred over corn tortillas. The diet is still high in fiber and complex carbohydrates. A rural existence encourages simple diets and increased activity. Exercise is a function of daily life where people walk to tend their fields and animals; they hand sow and harvest their crops and gather wild foods and craft-related plants. People walk to visit relatives and friends. One might see a Rarámuri walking while drinking a Coke, but such a picture would not be the norm.

Spanish explorers to northwest Mexico noticed the abundance of indigenous foods. When Cabeza de Vaca and his three lost companions stumbled through the area in 1534 and 1535, they came across people consuming corn, panic grass, amaranth, chenopods, squash, cactus, mushrooms, chilis, mesquite, acorns, yucca, piñon nuts, and beans. Cabeza de Vaca's journal entries reveal their surprise and pleased stomachs at the abundance that was being harvested by the Yoeme, Mayo, Jova, Opata, Pima, Guarijio, and Rarámuri. Food was of such variety that the people had time to experiment with and develop a specified way of preparing and cooking the varieties of available ingredients. They found uses for and made dishes devoted only to green corn. Of course, they waited for corn to dry on the stalk in the fields, after which it was ideal for storage and could later be ground into flour for foods such as tamales, tortillas, and gorditas. Sometimes, it would be roasted first and then ground into flour to alter its flavor and texture. Today, we call this pinole. Corn was even reconstituted and put into stew-like dishes along with beans and other ingredients. Some might regard the specified manner devoted to preparing corn a cuisine unique to

North America. The descendants of the people that Cabeza de Vaca shared meals with continue the relationship with foods that their ancestors established. In many ways, Native foods are the original American cuisine, which is fortunately very nutritious.

Beans, the second most consumed food in northwest Mexico, offer another view of how people enhance the diversity of their landscapes through foods. Most beans are identified by their botanical names as *Phaseolus vulgaris*. The common bean is the most abundant, comes out of its dried shell in many different shades of colors, and often is multicolored. In northwest Mexico, however, people also grew lima beans (*P. lunatus*), scarlet runner beans (*P. coccineus*), tiny wild beans (*P. metcafii*), and tepary beans (*P. acutifolius*). A North American hiker and writer traveling through the Sierra Tarahumara once asked a Rarámuri what the secret was of his people's endurance and good health. Apparently, the local man dashed off and then soon returned with a bag of beans. The high fiber, complex carbohydrates, low-fat soluble and insoluble fibers, and mucilages found in beans help to control glucose and insulin levels. Together, these nutrients and compounds serve the regular eater of beans with ways in which to avoid obesity and to keep cholesterol low. Just as tasty and nutritious as beans are cucurbits, also known as squash. They were and remain very important and also come in a variety of species such as *Cucurbita mixta* and *C. argyrosperma*, otherwise known as Cushaws. Warty squashes (*C. moschata*) are grown, as are blusher (*C. maxima*) and pumpkins (*C. pepo*).

If the indigenous diet of northwest Mexico had to rely on only the foods mentioned so far, the diets would be limited, yet still nutritious. Fortunately, many other wild foods are available, such as wild and domesticated chilis. Saguaro fruits and other cactus fruits remain a favorite, as is te de laurel. Te de laurel is an endemic tea found and consumed nowhere else but in the Sierra Tarahumara and by expatriates from the region who have managed to bring the leaves of this fragrant tree to other parts of Mexico and into the United States. Like the bay laurel tree that grows in northern California, the leaves are very fragrant and can be used in cooking. Unlike the bay laurel, the smaller variety of te de laurel that grows along the canyon walls of the deep Barranca del Cobre is less bitter and ideal for a refreshing and relaxing tea.

The indigenous diet is largely vegetarian, but this does not mean animal protein is not used or is shunned. In the past, people hunted and consumed deer, javalina, wild fowl, rabbit, and pocket gophers. Today, chicken, turkey, goats, and beef are eaten, which marks a degree of assimilation to foods introduced by Europeans. Assimilation can be marked by the amount of modern foods found in the diet. As people move to the mestizo towns and as the towns and tourism industry move toward the rural villages, the amount of modern foods increases, along with high-fat and low-fiber foods. Still, the diet remains close to what was eaten by Native peoples in this region over 300 years ago, and people's relationship to place retains its kincentric flavor.

When the people speak of the land, the religious and romantic overtones so prevalent in Western environmental conversation are absent. To us, the land exists in the same manner as do our families, chickens, the river, and the sky. No hierarchy of privilege places one above or below another. Everything is woven into a managed, interconnected tapestry. Within this web, there are particular ways that living things relate to one another. All individual life plays a role in the cycle. One Rarámuri elder mentioned to me that "It is the reason why people should collect plants in the same way that fish should breathe water, and birds eat seeds and bugs. These are things we are supposed to do."

Rarámuri land management and resource use are harmonized with ecological ethics that positively affect the local environment. The Rarámuri understand that cultural survival is directly linked to biological survival of the Sierra. Over the centuries, methods of land use were developed that adhered to this understanding. Horticultural and agricultural techniques included selective coppicing, pruning, harvesting, gathering, incipient management, cultivation, transplanting, vegetative propagation, sowing, discriminate burning, and weeding.

For the uninitiated, these are relatively technical terms used by ecologists, ethnobotanists, and conservationists to describe the various means by which people manage local landscapes. Coppicing refers to small-scale cutting back of vegetation such as bushes. For example, Ute Indians still cut back certain stands of willow to near the soil level during the winter months in order to promote straight and even growth in the spring. Coppicing works also as a means of population control of certain plant species. Pruning is similar to coppicing, except the practice is focused on cutting back only portions of the plant, normally to promote new growth of food-bearing plants such as oaks and berry plants. Harvesting and gathering are relatively familiar terms, but incipient management is used by those in this field to describe land management that was not the result of a grand plan or strategy, but appeared as a result of culturally sanctioned rules regarding the collection of the products of the landscape.

American Indians propagated some species of plants in order to select for certain characteristics, which is known as vegetative propagation. The best example in this context is when we speak of the introduction of Old World fruit plants such as apples and peaches to North America. Today, many Hopi still trade grafted peaches from the various surviving orchards among the Hopi Mesas.

Gathering techniques, such as that of collection of basket materials, have enhanced the functioning of ecosystems for centuries. These actions have influenced the diversity of species at a morpho-physiological, ecological, and even evolutionary level. Through intentional and incipient plant dispersal, alteration of the forest with controlled burning, and selective pruning and coppicing, the Rarámuri have contributed to the quality and functioning of the environment. These practices affect the reproduction of plant populations by modifying genetic compositions and species interactions. This is logical and easy to comprehend when it is understood that Rarámuri cultural priorities are also ecological and, therefore, hold the world together for the people as well as the animals and plants.

Very little of the North American continent has been untouched by humans. Except for some of the loftiest peaks and hottest desert locations, the land has been managed just like a garden. And in most places where people have sustainably lived with their place, the diversity of the place has been enhanced by the practices of the people. Today, this wild sort of mutualism lives on. In the Sonoran Desert, Sandfood and the Hia-Ced O'odham have sustained a pleasant symbiosis. Where willow and sumac abound, indigenous basket makers have found a way to ensure their materials will always be there through careful pruning. Juniper trees across the South-west provide bow staves without having to be killed. Camas root in British Columbia offers an example of mutualism that increases the wild crop. Traditional salmon weirs in northern California enhance the species. Native Californians burn the understory of oak groves, which decreases competition and increases the harvest. The Rarámuri carefully select the middle-sized onions to save the old ones for new propagation and the young ones for future bulbs. The collection of pine needles for weaving baskets is performed in a way that sustains the yield, while Yucca leaves are cut from the center of the plants to sustain the plant and its harvest.

Rarámuri land management represents a tradition of conservation that relies on a reciprocal relationship with nature whereby the idea of *iwígara* becomes an affirmation of caretaking responsibilities and an assurance of sustainable subsistence and harvesting. It is a realization that the Sierra Madres is a place of nurturing that is full of relatives with whom all breath is shared.

Cultural survival can be measured by the degree to which cultures maintain a relationship with their bioregions. Ecologists and conservation biologists today recognize an important relationship between cultural diversity and biological diversity. Cultural evidence for these relationships includes land-influenced language patterns that can be found in normal speech or in song and oratory. An example of this phenomenon was reflected in the Rarámuri example of referring to plants in terms of ethnicity and as relatives. Rarámuri *yúmari* and dutuburi songs that normally make references to flowers highlight another example. Associated with the flower references are referents to the landscape of the Sierra Tarahumara. In addition, ceremony and ritual drama intended to honor the land and to increase its abundance are an important part of the land–human relationship. Specific religious beliefs, such as land-based entities and forces, are equally important. Folklore, stories, and cultural history intimately describe specific bioregions as places to which the culture relates. The interior landscape reflects the indigenous relationships to their lands. The maintenance of the cultural landscape is an essential part of cultural survival.

When the language disappears, the sum of cultural cognition of the landscape is lost. In the Rarámuri language, images of nature are prompted by words and phrases. References to the process are heard in names of plants, songs, oratory, and metaphors. Encoded in the language is the Rarámuri inclination to seek nurturing relationships with nature.

The knowledge passed through a generation is practical knowledge that will eventually become sacred. During the intergenerational discourse, the metaphors and cultural models of plants as relatives and as humans develop and are intuitively understood. At this time, the younger ones will begin to comprehend the link between the notion of *iwígara* and the interaction of all life. The scope of Rarámuri ecology is only reinforced through ceremony, land management practices, and language. Ceremonies are performed expressions of Rarámuri ecology. Through the songs, oratory, and drama, Rarámuri ecology is revisited, performed, and reinforced among the participants.

Cultural histories speak the language of the land. They mark the outlines of the human–land consciousness. Under my grandfather's fig tree, I learned not only our cultural history but also the centuries of practical and spiritual knowledge that has evolved over a vast stretch of time that acknowledges our relationship to a place.

3

Pojoaque Pueblo and a Garden of the Ancients

"THEY DON'T KNOW why they're dancing anymore," Herman Agoyo sadly said. This was in response to my question of why he remained remorseful despite just telling me and my students that more young people than ever were returning to their village of low flat-topped adobe buildings in order to participate in the annual ceremonial cycle of dances at Ohkay Owingeh, formerly known as San Juan Pueblo. Like other Pueblos in northern New Mexico, elders and clan leaders at Ohkay Owingeh had been watching young people's participation and attendance at their dances drop over the last decades. The youth were drawn away to schools and jobs in Albuquerque and other cities across the Southwest. Then, Agoyo, a former governor of his community, had noticed attendance by young tribal members rise during the last couple of years. But they were coming only to wear the colorful and symbol-packed costumes during the dances, and not returning to live among the cottonwoods and earth-colored community along the Rio Chama just north of Espanola, New Mexico. Agoyo was especially full of lament that the youth were not returning to farm the dry and barren fields irrigated by the nearby river. According to Agoyo, one dances in order to pray for rain so that the crops can grow. He suggested that because the kids were not farming, they did not know why they were dancing.

Figure 3.1 Ancestral Puebloan petroglyphs; near Little Colorado River area in northern Arizona.

The act of Native agriculture involves much more than knowing when to plow, how to irrigate, and at what depth to sow seed. The responsibility of growing food for one's community is connected to one's identity as a member of the community. This identity, this sense of "being-ness," is tied to the history of the people on a land-scape. The very essence of being Ohkay Owingeh means that one's being is connected to the mountains that house the land on which the community survives. One's blood flows because the rivers and streams that flow across this landscape eventually feed the food that one eats. There is a consciousness that one exists because others came before who reaped this land and that others before them emerged from the very land, water, and air with which one still comes in contact. Raising an ear of corn in this context is a meta-phor for helping the children of the community grow and survive. Farming is a performance art that reflects one's relationship to place, the cosmos, and the community. If young people are only dancing and no longer is farming, then the behavior akin to making tortillas without flour or corn masa; the most important ingredients are missing.

There are sixteen Puebloan communities strung along the meandering path shaped by the Rio Grande and some of its tributaries as they flow across the arid land. The northernmost is the Tiwa-speaking community of Taos. Just south of Albuquerque, New Mexico, is the southernmost and Keresan-speaking community of Isleta. In between are Tewa-, Tiwa-, and Keresan-speaking Pueblos including Jemez, Zia, Santa Ana, Sandia, Ohkay Owingeh, Cochiti, San Ildefonso, Santa Domingo, Santa Clara, Nambe, Tesuque, San Felipe, Picuris, and Pojoaque. Each of these Pueblo communities was established centuries before the formation of the United States and the arrival of the Spaniards to what is today the American Southwest. According to archaeologist Mark Varien, "There are archaeologists who work in the Rio Grande who have recently found much greater evidence of developmental period settlement in the Rio Grande, so some of the Rio Grande Pueblo populations were likely there quite early, at least by AD 900 and perhaps earlier."[1] According to current research by Scott Ortman, some of the contemporary Pueblo communities trace their own community origins to earlier Pueblo communities that were strewn over a vast area, including the famous settlements to the north and west such as the pueblos of Mesa Verde, Chaco Canyon, Aztec, and Salmon. Ortman argues in his work "that the central Mesa Verde region was inhabited by Tewa speakers, at least between AD 1000 and 1300, and that they migrated and founded what we know today as the Tewa pueblos."[2] Each Pueblo maintains a unique character and history, yet while the ancestors of today's Pueblo speakers spoke languages representing five distinct linguistic families, they held one thing in common: they were all dry land farmers. But it appears that some communities along the Rio Grande were practicing irrigation agriculture before the Spanish arrived.

Anthropologists divide the technical and cultural processes of American Indian history into distinct phases based on art, pottery, material cultural remains, and subsistence. The first is the Archaic Era dating from 8000 BC to 1200 BC. These nomadic people traveled in small bands, gathering the wild foods of the region and hunting rabbits, deer, antelope, and bighorn sheep with throwing sticks, atlatls, darts, and stone-tipped spears. Small-scale cultivation began around 2000 BC along with a trend toward being more sedentary. During this era, Native people farther south, in what is now southern Mexico, were already hybridizing maize. By 7000 BC, early Mexicans were growing beans, peppers, pumpkins, and gourds. The early Mexican farmer–geneticists began experimenting with maize somewhere around 6500 BC near Puebla, Mexico. On the backs and side bags of traders, the grain made its way north, and by 1200 BC, gardens of maize along with squash were being planted by Native people in the Four Corners region. Their era continued until around AD 50. They constructed incredible and hardy baskets, used stone manos and metates to grind corn, and continued to hunt while living seasonally in caves and in the open. Between 400 BC and AD 500, Native Southwesterners began to live in shallow pit houses and were storing foods in bins. More important, rock art dating back to this era provides evidence for the beginnings of a ceremonial structure, although it is likely that ceremony had materialized prior to this period. The people were beginning to link their identity and their morals to how they impacted the landscape.[3]

Beginning sometime in the AD 500s and lasting until about AD 750, the people had added cultivated beans to their larders along with clay cooking vessels in which to prepare them. They continued to eat maize as well as wild and semidomesticated plants including prickly pear, goosefoot, ground cherry, and purslane. They had replaced their atlatls and spears with more efficient bows and arrows and were also beginning to domesticate turkeys while continuing to eat rodents, deer, and rabbits. Their ceremonial, agricultural, and social structure was becoming more complex with the advent of specialized ritual spaces. Anthropologists toss around the notion of increasing social and political complexity when they speak of early Southwestern history. *Complexity* has become a buzzword used to refer to the dizzying array of systems that early peoples must have relied on in order to solve problems, including problems associated with dry land farming in the face of ongoing droughts. This array includes their technology, social relations, symbols, and language. In other words, researchers are startled by the Pueblo ability to remain resilient in the face of rapid change at varying complexities.

Between AD 750 and 1300, the communities grew in several ways. Agricultural systems expanded and became more complex with the addition of terracing and irrigation in some locations. Social integration and religious societies grew during this period. The population increased and people began to live in their pueblos year round. By the early AD 1000s, Chaco Canyon, in present-day northwest New Mexico, had become a regional center of trade and ceremony. Pueblo people living there built great houses that were as much as four stories tall and contained several hundred rooms; and they constructed great kivas that spanned 50 to 70 feet. Over 200,000 timbers used to build these structures were transported from great distances. Chaco declined as a regional center by about AD 1150. Population grew in other areas, including the northern San Juan region, where sites such as Salmon, Aztec, and the famous cliff dwellings of Mesa Verde National Park are located; however, by AD 1300, these communities in the Four Corners were also devoid of people.

Drought was a persistent problem for Pueblo farmers, and a long and persistent drought that dated from about AD 1140 to 1180 was especially challenging for Pueblo people. This persistent drought challenged their agricultural systems, bringing stress to the increasing complexity of the social systems. During the Chaco Synthesis project sponsored by R. Gwinn Vivian, we discussed whether the observed complexity in the social systems and religious fervor might actually have been a result of the people's attempts to appease whatever supernatural forces that could have been causing the rain to stop coming to the dry landscape. In any case, the people left and founded new communities along the Rio Grande River, at the tops of mesas at Acoma and Hopi, and near more reliable sources of water at Zuni and Laguna. It must be stated here that although the 1140–80 drought certainly played a large role in the decline of Chaco, later droughts added to the resulting depopulation of the Four Corners region. After Chaco, according to Mark Varien:

There was considerable population growth in the northern San Juan region. This population peaked during the 1200s, at

the same time there were many environmental challenges, including some resource depletion (e.g., wood and large game
and probably some soil nutrient depletion), several periods of
colder-than-normal temperatures which impacted growing
seasons, several droughts (including the "Great Drought of
1276–1294," and arroyo cutting that began in the late 13th
century). These environmental challenges combined with dra-
matic population growth led to increasing conflict. This was
the social and environmental context of the 1200s that led to
the depopulation of the Four Corners country.

Nevertheless, the modern-day descendants of those that migrated don't normally speculate as to why their ancestors moved
away from the Four Corners region. Once I heard Peter Pino,
former governor of Zia Pueblo, whose community is tied to what
is now called the Mesa Verde region, express that "it was simply
time to move on." Pino also suggests that when the people began
to migrate into the Rio Grande Valley, it was not very different
from when American setters began to migrate to the West. He
says that the people sent scouts into the area and then groups of
Pueblo settlers trickled into the area, reporting back to the ones
that remained in the Four Corners region. Pino also suggests that
Pueblo people are curious and had a desire to "go south." In fact,
he suggested that, had it not been for the Spanish Entrada of
1598, Pueblo people would have continued to migrate south, following the course of the Rio Grande and founding communities
along the way.

Often when archaeologists refer to the early Puebloan eras, they
apply the term *complex* to the evolving social structures. There is a
Pueblo I complex followed by a Pueblo II and then a third complex. It is as though the temporal divisions had morphed into elements of matter and were locked in space. What was once a way of
being on a landscape is now a thing; a noun to be debated by people that never lived the culture, not even today's evolution of it.
But this is simply not the case. There are no past or present societies simple enough to be pickled into a space–time continuum in
order to be relegated to a complex. All societies demonstrate a
complexity and dynamic quality unique to themselves. And anthro-

pologists recognize this. The Pueblo I–IV titles are only markers that help researchers better perceive that evolution of American Indian complexity and change in the Greater Southwest. Herman Agoyo's problems reflect the process of complexity whereby social change is occurring in reaction to both internal and external factors beyond anyone's control in the community. This is not a new phenomenon in the history of Herman's culture.

Beginning around AD 1350 and stretching to the present era, the Pueblo communities were normally built around central plazas, black-on-white pottery gave way to red, orange, and yellow; and some of the people began to grow cotton as a resource as well as a commodity. By the 1500s, the Pueblo people found themselves sharing their landscape with newcomers such as the Navajo and Apache. Conflicts arose as a result of the newcomers, but there were examples of cooperation and even trade. During the sixteenth century, a new crop of newcomers would arrive. These folks proved to be less cooperative and would bring conflict and impacts never before experienced by the Pueblo people.

Intense adaptation and stubborn resilience have characterized Pueblo society since the arrival of the Spaniards during the sixteenth century. Every facet of Pueblo society and culture has been threatened and impacted since the period when Franciscan missionaries broke into kivas in order to destroy carvings of kachinas because they felt them to be evil idols. The atrocities are too numerous to document; but while Spanish military leaders were cutting off the feet of Pueblo men who refused to submit to the religious and civil edicts, Spanish farmers were arriving to the area. These settlers had little concern about whether their Pueblo neighbors were idol worshipers. All they desired was irrigated land into which they could introduce Old World and Mesoamerican (the geographic and cultural region between the North and South American continents) crops, the seeds of which they carefully brought with them from the south.

Spanish agriculturalists introduced watermelons, peaches, apricots, apples, cherries, oats, wheat, and livestock such as sheep, cattle, and goats. Chili is a staple at nearly every traditional Pueblo meal. And while many suggest that the Spanish also introduced the pungent condiment to indigenous people in the American South-

west, others find this difficult to accept. Chili is native to the New
World. It is very likely that it was traded from the south along with
the numerous macaw feathers, seashells, and other elements formerly found only in Mesoamerica.

Despite the atrocities and introduced crops, the remnants of
Pueblo agriculture resemble the systems that were in place before
the arrival of the Europeans. At Hopi, the sandy soils of the dry
washes in between the mesas and the dry soils at the shoulders just
below the mesa walls continue to nourish maize of various colors.
One can still find waffle gardens and large fields managed by several
families at Zuni Pueblo. Farmers at Tesuque just planted 750 fruit
trees and plan to grow 50 varieties of heirloom beans. Across Highway 285 at Pojoaque Pueblo, a group of visionaries are planning to
plant the Garden of the Ancients as a way both to revitalize Pueblo
agriculture and to feed their people from the landscape.

One of the central visionaries for Pojoaque Pueblo's Garden of
the Ancients is Vicente Roybal. We first met outside of the Poeh
Cultural Center and Museum at the Pueblo. The Center is the
Pueblo's new showcase cultural center, museum, governor's office,
and art school beautifully molded into New Mexico Pueblo–style
architecture, which resembles what some of the religious buildings
at Chaco or perhaps Mesa Verde might have looked like. At first
meeting, Vicente appeared a serious man, but his firm handshake
and warm smile quickly made me feel welcomed. It was a warm
spring day in northern New Mexico as we stood outside the Center, admiring both the stonework of the new buildings and the rug-
ged yet inviting landscape that makes New Mexico so enchanting.
The sound of grinding machines and steel chisels shaping rock
collided with rock music on a radio. Vicente pointed out a sculpt-
ing program that was going on as a part of the Poeh Center's mission to train Native artists. As we stepped inside the building, the
warm day was abruptly replaced with cooler and more humid air-
conditioning. Vicente explained that the Center's museum maintains a large collection of Native art and artifacts that require a
steady temperature and humidity. I was reminded of my curatorial
days at the Heard Museum in Phoenix, Arizona, when I would
sometimes eat my lunch outside in the 110-degree heat just as a

way to breathe real air and to remind my sinuses that they normally had 15 percent arid desert air passing through them.

Vicente and I were informed that the governor, with whom we were scheduled to meet, was running late. Vicente suggested that we use the time to look at the museum's centerpiece exhibit. We walked down a narrow hallway toward and through what seemed like the opening of a cave. It felt as though we were entering a portal into another dimension. First, the sound of water strikes the senses, and then the eye is led to several figurines of Native hunters outside in a snow-covered landscape. The figures are dressed in skins fringed with fur and carrying hunting implements such as atlatls and spears. What also piqued my attention was that the figurines resembled very short, round, wide-eyed dark-skinned people with huge round feet. For some reason, I was reminded of Hobbits in the *Lord of the Rings* films, but these Hobbits didn't have fur on their feet. Vicente explains that the artist who made the figurines was none other than Roxanne Swentzel, a renowned Native sculptor from the nearby Santa Clara Pueblo. A trough of water flows the entire length of the exhibit, as the visitor is led through a history of the Pueblo. It begins with the emergence from a *Sipapu*, past early hunting and gathering days, through the beginnings of agriculture, through the Spanish Entrada, and then, finally, into the living room of a modern-day Pueblo family home where a boy sits on the floor with a television remote in his hand as he watches a big-screen TV.

This last scene was the most profound for me. On the walls and on the floor were reminders of the almost daily struggle that Pueblo and other Native people endure as their Native self collides with the one that understands iPods, traffic jams, and foreign war. The big-footed boy sits on a handwoven rug perhaps of Navajo origin. On the side tables near the television are sepia-tone photos of ancestors or grandparents that are wearing military uniforms. On the walls next to modern photos and art hang ceremonial regalia and the head of a deer with strands of turquoise hanging around its neck and prayer offerings dangling from it antlers. The scene could have been the living room of many of my Pueblo friends. Change the ceremonial regalia and add Christian icons, and the living room might belong to a traditional Hispano family in northern New Mexico.

Ethnicity and identity are human constructs that individuals and communities constantly reinvent, reaffirm, and reconstruct. The process involves every facet of what we humans rely on to remind us of who we are and where we come from. In addition, we use food, art, music, dance, clothing, our language, and even the way we walk as symbols that we can grasp at when our identity is shaken. At Pojoaque Pueblo, what there was to grasp at was nearly all wiped out—twice.

At one point in Pueblo history, Pojoaque was the place from where the Tewa-speaking people dispersed as they founded other Tewa communities such as Nambe, Tesuque, and Santa Clara. The name *Pojoaque*, which, in the Tewa translation, means "water drinking place," denotes the historical importance of the location. Today, a little over 2,000 people live at the Pueblo. The Pojoaque Pueblo has risen from near extinction into a thriving economic and cultural center that is a tribute to its leader's creativity and resilience. Pojoaque is a model for cultural revival and survival.

When Vicente and I exited the exhibit, it was time to meet the governor. We climbed upstairs, landing at a large outer office. Standing in this outer office was an older gentleman with white hair that rested in stark contrast to his dark skin. I was reminded of my father and one of my older brothers, both of whom have white hair and dark skin. Vicente introduced the man as Amalio Madueño, the Poeh Center's development director; yet Vicente spoke the man's last name so quickly that I didn't really hear it the first time. Amalio was dressed very neatly in khaki pants and a buttoned-up shirt. As we shook hands, his smiling expression shifted to one of a man squinting in deep thought while he repeated my last name a couple of times and said, "You know, I have a cousin named Eddie Salmon." I replied, "I have an older brother named Eddie Salmon." I recalled Amalio's last name and said, "Madueño; my Mom's maiden name was Madueño." We studied each other's faces for a second, and then Amalio asked, "Is your mother Esperidiona?" I replied yes and realized that I was reviving a dormant relationship with a first cousin that I had not seen in nearly 40 years.

Many outside the larger Pueblo world describe the Pueblo of Pojoaque as having been extinct for decades, but those within suggest that Pojoaque was merely dormant. It was simply inactive until conditions were such that the community could revive. I once heard Peter Pino respond to the suggestion that Pueblo people had "abandoned" Mesa Verde with the countersuggestion that the community was not abandoned and that, in fact, Pueblo folks might return to Mesa Verde one day. Nonlinear conceptualization of time is one reason that Pueblo people remain resilient. As a result, the community of Pojoaque has become a model of indigenous reconnection and cultural and community renewal. We finally entered the governor's office, where I was introduced to young George Rivera, governor of Pojoaque, as well as Emigdio Ballon, cofounder of Seeds of Change, who is now working for Tesuque Pueblo as its agricultural director. I was also introduced to the ambitious and visionary Garden of the Ancients.

"Let's feed our own," is how Emigdio conceptualizes the plan. He had been brought onto the project as the spiritual and agricultural consultant. In the past, all the Pueblo communities fed themselves from the numerous fields that were once on the outskirts of the community. Mulch gardens on hillsides stored rain and runoff in the soil below the layer of riverbed gravel mulch. Fields were placed along washes to take advantage of the precious moisture trapped in the sandy loam, while other fields both near to and slightly removed from the central plaza relied on both rain and partial irrigation in order to grow the essential foodstuffs for the people. The Garden of the Ancients will return some forms of historic agriculture to Pojoaque, but will introduce large tracts of terraced crops and herbal gardens shaped into spirals. In a way, the Garden will be a work of sculpted and edible art.

Hobby farmers at many of the Pueblo communities have kept the long-term agricultural memory alive. They are mostly elder farmers mixed with younger community members that raise some heirloom and nontraditional crops. Some of the crops, such as blue and red corn, are used for ceremony and to supplement what people bring home from grocery stores. Some of the farmers manage to supplement their incomes by taking their crops to the growing number of farmer's markets springing up in Santa Fe and Albuquerque. A handful of restaurants also rely on greens and herbs that the farmers can produce. Nowhere, however, is anyone solely subsistent on the foods that they can grow in their own fields.

But the goal is not to become totally subsistent. This is near impossible today because Pueblo members must work outside of the community, leaving little time to toil in fields. It is possible, however, for a community to support a portion of the population that returns to farming in order to supply locally grown foods to a percentage of the population. In this way, a spiritual connection that has been absent from many Pueblo communities could return to the dinner tables. In addition, locally grown traditional foods could play an important role in stemming adult-onset type 2 diabetes, which is rampant among Pueblo community members.

Emigdio Ballon mirrors these sentiments. To him, growing food is equivalent to raising medicine for the community. He suggests that the foods themselves are medicine for both the soul and the body. He embodies his sentiments; he is a short man in his early 60s with a sinewy and strong physique that young twenty something athletes would envy. The life force of the northern New Mexico landscape is revealed in his eyes when he talks about the land and the foods that can be raised on it as our first source of healing. He maintains a seed bank of heirloom crops from across Native America and from Native communities reaching into South America. We originally met at a traditional Native peoples meeting nearly 20 years ago outside of Albuquerque. There, he had given me heirloom red, blue, and white seed potatoes from his homeland in the highlands of Bolivia. For three seasons, I grew and ate his potatoes while living in the San Luis Valley in south central Colorado. Under Emigio's spiritual approach to agriculture, Tesuque is now planting several acres of traditional and other food crops that are directed to the people in the community, who recently planted 750 fruit trees and are now growing 50 varieties of beans.

In addition to providing foods to the communities, these projects serve to expand and enhance the diversity of the landscape. Emigdio insists that his Tesuque workers maintain a low impact on the fields. They use hand tools, which Emigdio somehow manages to bring north from Bolivia, to weed and aerate the soil. During one visit, he demonstrated a planting stick comprised of a stout-looking wooden pole about 5 feet tall with a sharp metal point mounted at one tip. Native agriculture has mostly been low impact. It has normally worked in concert with systems that mimic natural processes. As a result, soils maintain their nutrient value and, most important, their microfungi, which act to bind and rebuild soil nutrients. Native farmers have always allowed and often encouraged weedy plants to grow at the edges of and sometimes within the fields. These plants are not really weeds, however. Most of them are useful edible greens and medicinal plants. I have identified 151 species of useful plants at the edges of the acequia feeding Hispano fields in northern New Mexico. Around Hopi Pueblo fields, one can often dig up the thick-skinned tubers of curly dock and find several varieties of chenopods, also known as lamb's-quarters. Many of the plants that find their way to the edges and among the rows of traditional fields tend to be edible greens of one sort or another. Discerning a "weed" from a useful plant is often tricky because one culture's weed is another's medicinal plant. A friend, ethnobotanist Karen Adams, once explained to me that a "weed is just a useful plant with a bad press agent." Still, it is important to be able to distinguish a weed or a useful plant from a planted crop.

One early summer, my ethnobotany students and I were exchanging some labor in Eric's field for his letting us camp on his land and listen to his stories. The students were working tirelessly, hoeing weeds among the rows of young corn. Most of the corn plants were about a foot tall and already easily distinguishable from the many weeds popping up among them. Still, Eric had made certain to show the students which plants were weeds and which were not. At one point in the work, Eric came over to me and some of my students and began telling one of his many intriguing stories about Hopi life. All the students took advantage of the event to take a break from their work to listen. All except one. She continued to work about 50 feet away. Her long blond dreadlocks splayed across her bent-over back as she vigorously chopped away at the weeds. In the middle of his storytelling, Eric glanced over at the dread-locked laborer, and his face instantly switched from its usual graceful smile to one of wide-eyed horror. He moved quickly over to the perspiring student, regained his composure, and in a most gracious manner informed her that she had just cleared away about

30 feet of his corn. Then her face took on a look of horror. She apologized profusely while Eric took the opportunity to use the moment for another story. The student later went on to be one of my best ethnobotany majors, and last I heard, she was managing the produce section of an organic foods grocery.

Traditional Native fields appear less uniform than their modern relatives that are planted in Iowa and in the Central Valley of California. They might actually appear overgrown and neglected. The result, however, is a diversity of plants in and around the fields that serve to keep the soils and planted crops from becoming overheated. In addition, the diversity of plants attracts pollinators and the birds that try to eat them. Rodents and small mammals approach the fields as well as welcomed snakes that feed on the rodents. In this scenario, repeated throughout Native America, traditionally planted fields offer green mosaics that create ecosystems and microhabitats. A Native field is a diversity condo that can be eaten.

Diversity is beneficial not only for the natural world but also for the human one. Cultural diversity manifests in the hundreds of languages spoken around the world and by the traditional knowledge of managing landscape encoded in those languages. It is important to remember, however, that none of the populations that speak the various languages ever lived in isolation; each had contact with many other peoples. From this contact, ideas and innovative ways of doing things were shared and evolved. Clayton Brascoupe, a transplanted Mohawk Indian who married into Tesuque Pueblo and became a well-known farmer in the Southwest, reminded me of this when he was speaking to me about Slow Food's Terra Madre celebration in Torino, Italy. We were standing at the edge of Tesuque Pueblo's agriculture project fields. About 20 acres of land on the reservation had been set aside for growing traditional foods that provide foods to the schools, the elderly, and the participating families still on the Pueblo. It was a typical sunny late winter day in northern New Mexico. Our feet became caked with layers of mud, even though we were careful as we walked among the irrigated rows. The sky illuminated with that deepest of sky-blue colors, or what one old friend and longtime New Mexico resident called "New Mex Blue." The horizon was shaped by the leafless cottonwood trees along the riverbank and by the Jemez Mountains in the distance. Some of the peaks were sprinkled with snow.

Clayton kicked at the ground with his hands in his pockets. He looked up at me and began to tell me about how "awesome" Terra Madre was. He spoke like a little boy telling his best buddy his memories of his very cool summer vacation. At one point, Clayton said that he never realized how being a "simple farmer" could be so special to other people. For nearly 22 years, Clayton has been the director of the Traditional Native American Farmers Association (TNAFA), a very loose coalition of Native farmers who come together to share traditional knowledge and seeds, hold permaculture classes, and offer summer youth internships on Native farms. The organization is a very low-tech enterprise. It doesn't even have a Web site, and getting ahold of Clayton through e-mail is a gamble. He prefers to meet people in person or to speak with them on the phone. In North America, TNAFA is not very well known except for its scant funders and a handful of people interested in traditional farming, seed saving, and permaculture. This is why Clayton described his experience in Italy as unusual. He would be looking at an exhibit there and people, he said, "would just come up to me like they wanted to shake my hand or something. It was like I was a celebrity." It turns out that Europeans are deeply fascinated by and interested in Native farming and had been researching people and organizations such as Clayton's in order to learn more.

For those persistent few who are able to make contact with TNAFA and Clayton, the rewards are as rich as the bottomlands at Tesuque Pueblo. Under Clayton's leadership and vision, TNAFA has educated hundreds of indigenous and non-nation peoples about heirloom seed saving, holistic approaches to land management and agriculture, composting, irrigating in arid regions, and restoring lands to sustainability. Largely as a result of Clayton's and TNAFA's untiring work, the 2006 Seed Sovereignty Declaration was drafted in Alcalde, New Mexico. The opening line of the Declaration reads, "Whereas, our ability to grow food is the culmination of countless generations of sowing and harvesting seeds and those seeds are the continuation of an unbroken line from our ancestors to us and to our children and grandchildren." Perhaps it will require people in Europe to help people in North America to open our eyes to the importance of our surviving traditional Native farmers.

If people such as Vicente Roybal and the Pojoaque governor have their way, everyone in North America will soon understand the role that Native farmers play in our human food future. Pojoaque, for example, is the Pueblo that refused to die. This is partly because the community rebuilt what was left of its ceremony, ritual, and community traditions through borrowing customs from its Pueblo neighbors. Resilience results from cooperation and adaptation. Pojoaque adapted to its loss and shortcomings and to what fate had handed it. As a result, it has contributed to the mosaic of Native pueblos already surviving in northern New Mexico. Cultural mosaics correlate with diversity, adding to the cultural pantry in the region. Although outsiders and some Pueblo community leaders complain and chide Pojoaque about not being a "real" Pueblo, the historical fact is that the Pueblos have always cooperated and collaborated. Survival in the region has traditionally depended on cooperation.

When Pecos Pueblo suffered from disease and the effects of the Spanish Entrada, its inhabitants were invited to move in with their linguistic cousins at Jemez Pueblo. The leader of the Pueblo Rebellion of 1680, Pope, was from Ohkay Owingeh, but based the Rebellion out of Taos Pueblo. Today, the agricultural visionaries from Pojoaque have traveled to Peru to gain what they can from existing indigenous agricultural systems.

Pojoaque occupies a unique position in that the community will be able to push agricultural innovation primarily because it was nearly extinct. As the community reemerges, it is reinventing itself. Despite complaints and criticisms, its people are forging ahead and in the process are reinventing what it means to be an indigenous people in today's complex of globalized, McDonald's-ized, Wal-Martized, and politicized Native communities. Pojoaque is part of the new "indigenous-tude" that refuses to disappear and in reality is nothing really new. Like its ancestors that moved from the Four Corners region to the Rio Grande Valley, today's Pueblo, will be well prepared to migrate into the next level of resilience.

Notes

1. Personal communication with Mark Varien, January 7, 2010.

2. Scott G. Ortman, "Conceptual Metaphor in the Archaeological Record: Methods and an Example From the American Southwest." *American Antiquity* 65, no. 4 (2000):613–45.

3. For archeological reference, see Richard I. Ford, ed., *Prehistoric Food Production in North America*, Anthropological Papers, No. 75. Ann Arbor: Museum of Anthropology, University of Michigan, 1985, pp. 245–78

4

*We Still Need
Rain Spirits*

PERSISTENCE. AFTER A click of my computer mouse, a digital Webster's dictionary suddenly zooms onto my computer's desktop. The dictionary defines persistence as "firm obstinate continuance in a course of actions in spite of difficulty or opposition." After a brief contextual example in italics about companies and their need to have patience, an alternative definition is suggested, which states, "the continued or prolonged existence of something." Together, both definitions sum up Hopi existence. To be additionally specific, I would refer to Hopi persistence as resilient persistence. Hopi persistence is resilient because the Hopi have patiently figured out how to transform actions and behaviors that make sense into the sacred, and what is seen as sacred into practices that make sense. The most poignant example of this is seen in Hopi prophecy, which doesn't simply suggest a possible future path, but one that is unfolding daily and openly for everyone to see.

We were standing at the edge of Eric Polingyouma's cornfield, looking at a small collection of various sized rocks. For most of Eric's 70 plus years, he has coaxed heirloom Hopi crops from the sandy soils of the Colorado Plateau. He and his Hopi clan members and neighbors have relied on a time-tested process that pays homage and honor to the elements of land and sky as well as the unexpressed and unrecognizable dimensions of nature. One way to honor these forces is through shrines placed at the edge of agricul-

Figure 4.1 Hopi elder in cornfield; near Kykotsmovi, Arizona.

tural fields. Eric's shrine of rocks in no discernible order sat on the sandy soil. During a conversation in the prefabricated house that was Eric's home with his wife, Jane, he had asked if I wanted to see his shrine. We bent under the dry heat as we walked across the cornfield of several acres. On the way through the heat, I harbored a romantic vision of a shrine with colorful prayer sticks and something befitting of the sacred. The unadorned pile of stones was a bit of a disappointment.

Not more than 40 feet away was the steep edge of an arroyo that cut through the northern Arizona plateau country on what is now the Hopi reservation. The cut began about 20 miles to the north at the edge of Black Mesa, ran south and west through Eric's land under Highway 259, and disappeared into the distance toward Leupp, Arizona. Eric said the arroyo was relatively new. In fact, what is now an empty interruption of the landscape used to be a part of Eric's cornfield where he raised ten varieties of Hopi corn including red, blue, white, yellow, sweet, lavender, and what they call "greasy hide." Eric also grows beans and squash, and encourages semidomesticated medicinal and edible plants to flourish. The arroyo reflected the current and unusual aridity of the Colorado

Plateau and other parts of the American Southwest. For nearly 11 years, this area has been parched by an ongoing drought. In 2006, Arizona suffered the driest year on record.

The Hopi Way, as Jane and Eric often call their approach to life, is not one of outcome or product. What is important to them is the journey and what is learned along the way about their relationship to place and community. It is a way of resilient persistence. Some cultures have been able to successfully endure shocks to their social and environmental systems. They have accomplished this either by chance or through intentional social and communal design as a result of recognizing adaptations that have worked in maintaining their ways of life. Often, this happens overnight or through elongated temporal and spatial processes. For the Hopi, aridity, drought, and going without have been incorporated into their worldview and into their social, spiritual, and agricultural practices. Hopi origin tales, as well as Hopi prophecies, speak about issues that are increasingly becoming realized and reaffirm their persistence. In one humbling moment, I experienced firsthand a Hopi prophecy materializing.

I was in a Hopi community during the summer of 2000 at a time of ceremony. The Ogres[1] rustled around outside. Deep guttural growls echoed from inside the bellies of the creatures. The growls were expressions of the need for bad children to be sent outside so that they could be eaten. I sat in the interior of a centuries-old home near the center square where dancing and drumming could be heard. Inside the home, the air was heavy with scents and aromas of ceremonial foods. I could distinguish roasted corn, mutton, bean sprouts, and hominy. The light was thick with steam from the cooking. People both young and old rustled in and out of the small kitchen that also served as a living room. The old man that Eric had brought me there to meet sat quietly in an old wooden chair along the opposite wall of his house. His presence was one of stillness. He seemed to be a part of the 700-year-old wall he leaned on. I was placed at a small table across the room to be served stew and other foods. I sat for nearly 45 minutes, savoring the various dishes and sipping on Hopi tea while carrying on small talk with Eric. Without any warning, the old man began to stir. He looked in my direction, gesturing with one hand as he spoke. Eric translated that he was telling me that my presence was in fulfillment of Hopi prophecy.

As the chill that had run up and down my spine subsided, I listened intently as the elder explained that, according to Hopi prophecy, there would come a time when non-Hopi would teach Hopi how to be Hopi again. The elder was making a reference I applied to the fact that my students and I had been invited by Eric's kiva to engage in a plant restoration project. We had been asked to help transplant a handful of plants, including sand reed. By itself, sand reed is an insignificant plant that shoots upward toward the sky, normally around the many springs hidden on the Plateau landscape. It grows in clumps from the sandy soils, but really presents very little economic value, unless you are Hopi and planning to get married. It turns out that sand reed stems are the primary weaving material for reed mats woven into long rectangular shapes and used as a protective casing in which handwoven marriage mantas are held. The manta represents the groom's gift to the bride's family and seals the coming together of separate clans. Through marriage, Hopi clans are extended which interconnects them and strengthens Hopi society. Without the reed mats, however, the marriage ceremonies would suffer, removing one more link in Hopi culture, society, and survival. Unfortunately, the sand reed had been increasingly difficult for the elders that weave the mats to locate; thus the role and purpose of the restoration project comes into play.

Like many Hopi farmers, Eric still maintains traditional cornfields on the same small fields dating back approximately 3,000 years. Throughout the region, rock art and ruins retell the story of the early people that managed small fields of various kinds of crops, domesticated animals, and channeled rainwater to their fields and into small catchments. Eric can read rock art around the Colorado Plateau and into southern Mexico that tells the tale of a population of resilient people and their movements through the various landscapes that now comprise much of the North American continent.

One day, sitting in their home near Kykotsmovi, Eric was talking with me about Hopi culture, spirituality, and history. He is fit for a man his age and for a man that has suffered a heart attack. His dark and weathered face seems to be always presenting a smile to the world. When he speaks, he chooses his words carefully and often aims his words toward somewhere other than the person he is talking with. As the last member of the Bluebird Clan, it is his responsibility to maintain and retell the Hopi past. Often when people hear this they become concerned that the knowledge held by Eric will disappear when he dies. Eric and Jane do have a son and a daughter, but in the Hopi Way, clan knowledge is passed down through the mother's side of the family. Hopi is a matrilineal society. Therefore, Eric must pass his extensive historical knowledge through his own clan, which is connected to his sister. Unfortunately, she never bore a male child. Therefore, there is no one left after Eric. He doesn't act very concerned that no one will maintain this element of Hopi culture. He reminds me that the Hopi Way recognizes the impermanence of nature of which human actions are a part.

In the conversation, Eric talked about the movement of the "Mexicans" coming from the south and settling at Hopi. In other conversations, he had mentioned the Mexicans as well. I assumed that he was complaining about migrant workers or alien residents that were from Mexico and were settling around northern Arizona. During this particular conversation, however, it dawned on me that he was referring to a Hopi clan represented by his wife, Jane. The Mexican, or Sun, Clan was the last group of people to migrate north from what is now Mexico. Eric talks about Hopi history as if it happened only yesterday. According to Eric, the Hopi did not always occupy their arid part of the Colorado Plateau. They originated in southern Mexico and in other parts of Central America. Nevertheless, during the past, this group of related people began to move about, eventually heading north. Mindful speculation would suggest that along the way they met up with and exchanged botanical and agricultural knowledge with other tribal groups and communities.

As the people migrated, settled for a short while, and then migrated again, a library of traditional ecological knowledge (TEK) coevolved with their increasingly complex social system of clans and societies. The introduction of corn, which requires a minimum commitment of staying in one place for 3 months while it grows and matures, must have further stratified Hopi society. In other words, the Hopi were forced to find a place to call home for the long term. Hopi social cohesion is achieved through obligation to a clan. The clans are part of the Hopi moral landscape, which is a reflection of their shared kinship to each other and to their human and nonhuman community.

Until the relatively recent human past, people living in small-scale agricultural communities drew the majority of their resources from their immediate landscape. At Hopi, the aridity of the Colorado Plateau makes life very difficult, always on the edge of failure. Like other indigenous communities around the world, the Hopi have a relationship with the landscape that has evolved over time. At some point, the Hopi must have figured out which crops grew on their landscape and how to most efficiently ensure their survival. Over time and after years of observation, strategies were developed that ensured an annual harvest. The strategies became what might be called practical knowledge, which over time became sacred knowledge. Because a writing system had not been developed, the best way to maintain this knowledge was through story, songs, and ritual. In this way, the Hopi collective memory became something that remained alive as long as the Hopi Way of life persevered. Because the knowledge, and as a result the culture, is affected by the landscape, the land itself is perceived as the source of the knowledge. This library of knowledge doesn't just remind people how to grow corn and beans in an arid landscape. It also reminds people how to behave. It teaches them what is right and wrong, and gives them the knowledge of what it takes in order to preserve this way of life. The land has become a source of morals and values, which are rekindled each time a story is retold, when the corn dancers fill the plaza in one of the Hopi villages, and whenever unfolding prophecy makes itself obvious.

As a result, in order to preserve the community, the land must also be preserved. This direct correlation is something that many in the fields of ecological restoration, biology, and land management have, until very recently, failed to notice. A superficial understanding of this realization, by many in the ecological and land management communities, is that Native peoples for centuries had manipulated their local environments through various mechanical means such as pruning, burning, and gathering. As a result, they impacted their ecological systems. Many reports imply that such Native "manipulation" was accidental. A talk presented by Eric one evening as a part of the Society of Ethnobiology at a meeting in Durango, Colorado, implied the opposite.

For nearly two hours, Eric and three other Native panelists described the deliberate land management practices of their various tribal communities. Not only did they detail exact practices, they also described the social, cultural, and spiritual reasonings that have guided their actions. During Eric's portion of the panel, he described how for centuries the ancestors of the Hopi and of the present-day Hopi have struggled to make agriculture work on the arid and climatically harsh Colorado Plateau. He noted the constant practical and spiritual vigilance required so that the Hopi could continue to live in this region. His talk even implied how the Hopi ancestors purposefully chose their difficult way of life.[2] While Eric captivated the audience with his mystical presence, the irony of Hopi existence emerged: that they and their Navajo neighbors have struggled on an arid landscape while only a few hundred feet underneath their fields, the porous crust of the Earth rests, saturated with billions of gallons of pristine water. The Hopi and the Navajo have no access to the water except for a handful of natural springs that dot the landscape. During the question-and-answer period, a person asked Eric why the Hopi don't simply dig wells and use irrigation in order to ensure their harvests. Eric stood there for a minute while he pondered the question. Although he maintained the smile that he presents while in public, he had a puzzled look on his dark and weathered face as if to suggest that he could not believe that someone would ask such a question. Finally, he said, "If the Hopi had irrigation, we would no longer need the kachinas." The audience was both stunned and exhilarated by Eric's response. I believe a smattering of epiphanies ran through the listeners as well.

The simplest description of kachinas is that they are rain spirits. A key for the survival of many small-scale agricultural systems is that rain will reach their fields; hence, the need for a belief in rain spirits. Native farmers do not base the reasoning behind their farming techniques on empirically supported agro-scientific evidence. They make decisions based on a responsibility to culture, clan, family, and land. These elements coincide for Native farmers as easily as do salsa and tortilla chips; they make perfect sense. To irrigate for people that have always relied on and trusted kachinas means to deny everything that it means to be Hopi. Identity here is tied up with responsibility to one's clan, to ceremony, to family, and to the land. This realization places the Hopi in context with the universe and with the land that is seen as nurturing. On the Colorado Plateau, although the land appears harsh and unforgiving, it actually cares for and protects the people. Retold and repeated stories and ceremony remind the people of this paradigm. It is a worldview whereby the people believe that they emerged from the land and the land models responsible behavior with all living things. As a result, to lose the land is to lose one's flesh, to lose one's sense of well-being. Landscapes have the power to influence people's ideas about themselves because of the history that has unfolded on them. From the events, moral metaphors are formulated by the community's shared understanding. Moral metaphors extend into Hopi models of their landscape affecting their ecological actions.

During the many talks I have heard Eric give, he often gets around to discussing the notion that to the Hopi, corn is mother. Native people throughout the Greater Southwest share a similar belief. To these folks, corn is an article of sustenance as well as the basis for their being. Corn plays a vital role in all ceremony and is a focus of cultural and individual identity. This concept is not unfamiliar to me, because the one way that Native oral traditions work is through repetition of story. The result is that culturally agreed-upon ideas and concepts are repeated and learned until they become second nature. One warm afternoon in the summer of 2003, Eric and I were standing on a rooftop watching a kachina dance. We shared the roof with many others, but most people were Hopi. From this vantage point, I could look in all directions for miles. To the south and a bit west stood the San Francisco Peaks rising up from the land near Flagstaff, Arizona. They shaped part of the hazy horizon to the south, looking like the back of a camel. In the small plaza of the village, there were several kinds of kachinas moving about at intervals. This particular dance included a set of Mud Heads called *Koyemsi* in the Hopi language. Eric explained to me that they act as an assortment of messengers between the human and the spirit or kachina world. They also can possess magical and healing powers, according to Eric. During the dance, they help maintain the movements of the dancers and often interact with the people watching. Among the Mud Heads were some dancers that wore what appeared to be unshorn sheepskin vests. Eric pointed out that these particular dancers represented germination, or "sprouting kachinas." When Eric mentioned this, the concept both surprised me and made sense to me. When a community's survival depends on maintaining total connection with the intricacies of its environment, no detail is ever missed. And no detail is not recognized and treated as sacred. When the Hopi say that all life is sacred, they mean it. Even an action that is a natural part of emerging life is prayed to. In this case, it was the notion of germination. The concept then became formulated into one that implies that all parts of emergence and reemergence are significant. Corn is not simply mother. The continued cycles and codependence that humans have with growing corn is sacred. When Eric grows corn, a sizable portion of his blue corn is always reserved for blue corn that will be used in his clan's kiva[3] and in its rituals. This is because he has a responsibility to his kiva and clan. It is a responsibility that he meets unquestionably as a result of his worldview.

Unfortunately, Hopi traditional culture is in peril. Environmental degradation is endangering the flora, fauna, and water table in and around the Hopi reservation. The loss of biodiversity and water, largely due to mining, is leading to the gradual decline of traditional land ethics that harmonize Hopi use of the land with conservation of the natural world. When the practices of traditional land management stop, the ceremonies stop, as well does Hopi language and, as a result, the encoded ecological knowledge. Concerned researchers often suggest that perhaps Hopi and other Native cultural knowledge should be preserved through directed collection of specific ecological knowledge. These so-called "memory banks" can be stored for later retrieval when the desired time is met. Most Native people aren't comfortable with the idea of memory banking or preserving indigenous knowledge. It is perceived as something akin to pickling it. This is because they consider that the knowledge itself has being-ness. The knowledge is a life force stewarded by those that maintain it while they speak the language.

When it is transferred from person to person, a bond develops between the people, strengthened by the life of the information and by the shared linguistic meanings. In this manner, the memories remain alive as long as the people maintain them in situ. When, however, the knowledge is transferred to the static, literal, documented state, its life force dissipates. Separated from the contextual language, the cultural meanings are missing.

The knowledge, when preserved in situ, maintains the cultural meanings plus the models and metaphors that affect action and land management systems that are still practiced. People such as Eric are living refugia of traditional ecological knowledge. Unfortunately, with the speedy loss of elders such as Eric, coupled with language loss and threats to the landscape—such as what the Peabody Coal Mine is doing by altering the water table—the kind of relationship that the Hopi have with water and their land is also being altered. I wonder then, is the moral landscape changing as well?

In the early 1930s, Alfred A. Whiting recorded an immense body of Hopi plant and agricultural knowledge. By the late 1930s, the Hopi had built a sophisticated agricultural system based partly on dry land farming and semi-irrigation techniques. Terraces fed by hand and natural springs hung at the edge of some of the mesa-top communities. Some families relied on intermittent and often heavy summer rains to fill the washes and arroyos in between the mesas and on the flat areas away from the mesas to feed their fields. The result was a mosaic of endemic and sustainable agricultural practices and crops unique to the Colorado Plateau.

The Hopi continue to raise varieties of corn, squashes, beans, and semidomesticated greens. Most contemporary Americans have been in contact with blue corn through numerous brands of corn chips available on the market today. Hopi farmers also raise red, pink, yellow, white, multicolored, and black corn. Corn types are identified also by variety such as flint, hominy, and flour corn. Hopi beans are also as varied. Across the reservation during harvest time, one can visit the fields and see people collecting black beans, red beans, and practically every color bean of the rainbow. The same can be said for the variety of squashes. Like other human communities in direct contact with a landscape, the Hopi also gather edible and other useful plants from the arid Colorado Plateau. If one knows where to search, numerous berries and edible fruits can be found, from wolf berries to sweet desert hackberries. Many plant materials are collected to be used for basket making for both household and ceremonial items.

The Colorado Plateau is a fragile landscape. Tire tracks etched into the sandy soils by mountain bikes and off-road vehicles scar the landscape for years until the elements can slowly erase them. Hopi ancestors learned that their impact on the land is lasting and therefore must be light. Archaeological evidence in the Southwest focuses on how ancient people impacted their environment and used their resources. In some cases, archaeologists have argued that these impacts and resource depletion forced people to leave their communities. This may be true for some past communities, especially those that were the largest population centers. Examples might include Chaco Canyon in New Mexico and Snaketown just south of Phoenix. At Chaco, the past inhabitants are referred to today as ancestral Puebloans. These Pueblo people carried thousands of timbers from both the Chuska and San Juan mountains up to 100 miles away in order to build their great houses, including massive timbers that must have been needed for the roofs of their large ceremonial great kivas. Foods were transported into the ceremonial center on the backs of humans from outlying communities, taxing the agricultural system. Eventually, years of drought, perhaps coupled with internal warfare, forced the people to migrate to areas where today we find descendants still living in large agricultural communities. At Snaketown, the Hohokam people coaxed the Sonoran Desert to allow large-scale agriculture by constructing miles of canals and watering ditches. The system tapped the nearby Salt and Gila rivers to irrigate the fields. Numerous check dams controlled water flow. A mosaic of modern canals that follow to a large degree the Hohokam system still brings water to the desert city of Phoenix. The Salt River remains a source of water, but the canals also bring water from the Colorado River. During Hohokam times, however, every time it rained in the mountains, the source of their precious water, the water that flowed through their canals and ditches also carried loads of silt. Eventually, the check dams and ditches became overburdened with the silt and were no longer usable. Heavy rains and flash floods began to destroy their dams and canals and eventually their agricultural system. Like the Ancient Puebloans, the people left their large towns, and it appears they took on smaller scale desert lifestyles.[4]

If one walks this landscape with Mark Varien, a different view of the past is revealed. Mark is the vice president of programs at Crow Canyon Archaeological Center located at the heart of the Four Corners region near Cortez, Colorado. He's a quiet, unassuming man with sandy hair and blue eyes that squint when he peers across the Four Corners landscape as if to better spot the often hidden evidence of past human occupation. In his slow Texas drawl that originated in San Angelo, Mark tells a story of a people that deliberately cared for the fragile landscape. In this story, the people were careful not to overuse their local resources to the point where they migrated periodically sometimes as close as a half mile away in order to give the soils on which they were managing and growing foods, time to rest and restore.

There is no doubt, according to Varien, "that people can't help but impact their landscape and resources when they occupy an area." But Mark would suggest that resource depletion was not the primary reason that people left the area. Land use resource depletion is a complicated process, making generalization difficult. Varien suggests that people in the Mesa Verde most likely "did impact their landscape and overuse some resources, but the fact that they maintained some communities for as long as 300 years, and that by moving around the landscape that they inhabited the region for 700 years, indicates they did this in a way that was relatively sustainable."[5]

Researchers at Crow Canyon have been uncovering a human past that reveals sophisticated land management practices and concern for how inhabitants impacted the land. Check dams, in this case small ones, not only captured natural rainwater to be used later for watering small agricultural fields but also served to control erosion to even increase the depth of soils so they could plant on slopes that would not be used by today's farmers for agriculture. In the Rio Grande region, gravel mulch was laid on small fields in order to conserve the precious moisture caught in the soils and perhaps to extend the growing season. Waffle-shaped gardens with up to 15-

inch walls are still used at Zuni Pueblo today. They are constructed to hang on to whatever moisture was in the soil feeding the roots of the crops and collect water from rainfall. The high walls partially shade the soil from direct sunlight. Other land management techniques included raising turkeys for their feathers and for food.

Modern descendants, such as at Hopi, still rely on many of these techniques in order to grow the crops they have relied on for centuries. This means that the corn, beans, squashes, and other crops that traditional farmers raise have been tested for their durability and resilience. They have withstood drought, sometimes too much rain, early and late frosts, and various kinds of pests; and they can be planted in soils that are normally low in nutrients. The only drawback to these heirloom crops—crops that have been grown by the same community or farmer for many generations—is that they tend to be endemic, unique to a region, an ecosystem, or a certain climate. The wonderful thing is that many of these crops survive today in the fields of farmers such as Eric and have become foods cooked in small kitchens all around the Hopi reservation.

Both daily and ceremonial foods reflect their farming techniques as well as spirituality and the relationship to place. During one visit with Eric and Jane, I had brought with me several students from the small liberal arts college where I used to teach ethnobotany, ethnoecology, and traditional ecological knowledge. Earlier in the day, the students had toiled under the hot sun weeding Eric's field, breaking to hear stories that Eric eagerly told. He told stories about ancient Hopi, prophecy, farming, mixed with humorous anecdotes. The students sat in the shade eating up the stories like elementary school children. It's incredible, but no matter what our age, we still enjoy a good story. I think we share a primal urge to share memories as a way to mingle and reaffirm our suspicions and observations about what we know and suspect about the world and each other. Stories help human communities to restore and build upon our collective memory and library of knowledge. It is a continuum of our human legacy.

After working and listening to stories, Jane called us into their small home in order to prepare the meal we would all be sharing. Some of the food that would be served came from the very field that the students had been weeding. I think this knowledge added to the importance of their work and to their attention to doing it properly. As we entered their home, we made sure to shake off the sandy soil from our shoes and boots and tried to find a comfortable place to relax. There was about ten of us in all, making finding a place to sit a bit difficult. Jane called the female students willing to help with the preparation of the meal into the kitchen. She quickly and assertively told the young men that offered to help that their place was with the other men in the living and dining rooms. To Jane, the kitchen was the realm of women with little room for men. This was not a conservative antifeminist stance, but one that reflected centuries of Hopi gender roles. In most American Indian communities, traditional women's roles are viewed as equal to and sometimes more important than those of men. At Hopi, women reflect the core of the Hopi base metaphor, which is that corn is mother. Mothers and women are the foundation of Hopi life and everything that is done. To me, to be a mother is also to be a nurturer. At Hopi, the clan system remains vibrant due to a matrilineal system that passes down knowledge and kinship through the mother's side of the family. The clans determine the ceremonial cycle and who participates in it.

From the kitchen floated a mix of scents of corn meal mingling with desert herbs, and cooking lamb, which would serve later to be an issue with Jane. Little by little, the dinner began to appear on the dining-room table. Jane and the female students carried out plates of small tamales called *sumiviki*, bean sprout stew, thin rolled-up blue corn bread called piki, and fresh roasted green chilis. We happily sat down and began eating. The students and I were thrilled at this feast while Jane seemed pleased until she noticed that two of my female students sitting next to her were not eating the bean sprout stew. I noticed how she looked sideways and unpleasantly at them. Most traditional Hopi will not confront someone directly if they are displeased with their actions or words. They feel that it is not their place to stir up consternation and bad feelings among people and, as a result, disturb the community. However, I could tell that Jane was uncomfortable, and the schoolteacher in her obviously decided that there was a teachable moment present and she spoke. She asked the two students why they were not eating the bean sprout stew.

Bean sprout stew is served at the beginning of the Hopi kachina ceremonial cycle. Kachinas, the spirit beings that reside in the San Francisco Peaks near Flagstaff, Arizona, return to the Hopi mesas beginning around February. They are coaxed into returning with dance, songs, and things such as bean sprout stew. The beans are sprouted in the dark recesses of the semi-subterranean kivas that dot the mesa tops among the centuries-old homes and clan houses. Jane and Eric were offering a very special food by serving it to my students in the summer, and these two impertinent girls, in Jane's eye, were obviously being ill mannered by refusing to eat it. As soon as one of the students answered Jane's question by suggesting that they were vegetarians, I closed my eyes, exasperated, as I knew what was coming next. The student said that they both not only were vegetarians but also were so because they did not believe in eating living beings. Jane quickly, and without losing a beat, responded that "if us Hopi thought like that then we would starve to death." The table descended into silence. I notice that Eric's dark face was wrinkled into a closed mouth smile while he quietly chuckled. The two students under scrutiny looked stunned and perhaps a bit embarrassed at this unwanted attention. The remainder of my students looked on, waiting for the next movement in this teachable moment. Jane continued, saying that "to us everything is alive, the plants, the animals, and even the rocks." She stopped there, letting the students interpret the point she was trying to make. In little time, the two began to eat a small portion of the incredible stew, and the moment folded back into the very pleasant meal as it had begun.

In order to raise all these traditional foods, the Hopi employ an agricultural system many refer to as dry land farming. As Eric pointed out in Durango, Colorado, the Hopi do not resort to irrigation. Still, crops require water or at least some water in order to reach the stage of growth when they produce fruits and vegetables. Most Hopi crops, as well as those of other Pueblo and Colorado Plateau Native farmers, are raised along the bottoms of arroyos where periodic rain fed by floods affords a sort of risky substitute for irrigation. At places such as Moenkopi, the fields are planted near and under cliffs along the edges of the valleys where seepage from springs provides moisture or where the wash receives so much runoff that the soil remains moist below the surface.

Beans are also planted on the mesa tops in separate plots as are often squashes, melons, gourds, chilis, and other vegetables. These crops are seen planted in the corner of cornfields when the farmer's fields sit below the mesas and in the flat areas between the mesas. Fruit trees can be seen below the mesas growing from small angled sandy fields. Terraces still line the sides of First Mesa where some heirloom fruit trees survive.

Hopi planting is done in phases that correlate with the annual ceremonial cycle, which is a reflection of the agriculture system, and celestial phases. The result is that the Hopis begin planting around April and continue into June. In February, teams of elders and youth normally related by clan or kiva house descend into the various fields for clearing. In late March and into April, sweet corn, an early crop, is planted. From mid-April through July, various kachina ceremonies take place—first to welcome the kachinas home from their perch on the San Francisco Peaks and then to ensure that they stick around in order to bring the rains. In May, the main corn crops along with melons, beans, and squashes are put into the ground. If the weather cooperates, people are gifted with early apricots. By July and into August, the main occupation of most Hopi farming families is weeding, hoeing, and thinning of the corn plants. Again, if there has not been an early frost and the dust storms have been bearable, people are able to relish a harvest of early corn. By August, the main corn and bean crops are beginning to be harvested, dried, and stored. The harvest flows into September and October, accompanied by basket and butterfly dances that offer thanks for the fruits that the land has provided the communities that sit atop and among the three mesas.[6]

Not all Hopi communities follow the processes exactly as I have expressed them here. In fact, some communities and families no longer plant and harvest at all. The good news is that some communities that have postponed their annual agricultural cycles are attempting to restore them. Many Native communities have reached this juncture in their evolution. It is where foreign and outside economic and social forces produce shocks and threats in front of the community. At this point, the people are given choices, one of which is to absorb and adapt to the shocks and to learn from the mistakes they may have made along the way. The information they draw from that will help them make educated choices is the same knowledge they have been cultivating for centuries. It is the long-term and shared memory that they have generated from resiliently managing a lifestyle in their place. In some cases, the people must be reminded and reeducated concerning what they collectively know.

The Natwani Coalition, with the leadership of Andrew Lewis, Kelvin Long, Greg Glasco, and others, has tapped into the collective memory with the aid of a very non-Hopi medium: photos.[7] Lifestyle changes since the beginning of a wage economy in the 1960s, and easier access to urban areas such as Winslow, Flagstaff, and Phoenix, have struck a heavy blow to traditional Hopi farming practices. While the agricultural practices and lifestyle wither away in the dry Colorado Plateau air, few parents are encouraging their children to take on the traditional farming that has sustained the Hopi community for millennia. Because the growing of food plays a central role in the ceremonial Hopi kachina dances, the loss of agricultural activity threatens the very heart of the Hopi religion. In addition, lack of physical activity and reliance on junk foods and other nontraditional food habits have resulted in more than half of Hopi elementary school children being overweight or obese. Diabetes has become the tribe's most serious health problem, affecting more than half of Hopi adults, while the Hopi Way, with the people's identity as stewards of the land, is slowly being lost among the younger generation.

With support of Hopi tribal and community leaders, the Natwani Coalition has held Hopi Food and Agriculture Summits in the community of Kykotsmovi. The summits have helped to launch additional innovative programs. With the participation of more than 300 tribal members, the community has suggested initiatives such as the following: creating a summer farming program for youth to work with traditional farmers and assist with terrace garden restoration; developing a culturally based classroom curriculum to teach children about traditional foods, farming, and gardening techniques; increasing the use of traditional Hopi crops by having school children grow seedlings and graft traditional fruit tree varieties; and promoting locally produced foods in school cafeterias. A healthy foods initiative has been launched at a Hopi elementary school.

A pilot greenhouse has since been built at the Kykotsmovi youth center, and clan members are returning to Wepo orchard terraces. Youth work parties are helping to restore water flow and have cleared the terraces for planting. Seedlings from Hopi heirloom fruit tree cuttings have been planted to restore the ancient orchard. Despite such efforts, the road will be a long one. What has been lost over the past 40 years will not be easily regained. To help the people recall how they used to plant and care for the orchards, Andrew Lewis has initiated a Hopi agricultural photo program.

It turns out that anthropologists and other researchers during the height of fieldwork among the "dying" tribal peoples of the West took hundreds of photos that have been sitting in archives on museum and library shelves for the last century. The Natwani Coalition created an exhibit of photos that specifically focuses on Hopi agriculture from the previous century. These photos are displayed at the Hopi Cultural Center on Second Mesa in northern Arizona. The idea, simple in its implementation, was that Hopi community, both young and old, would see the photos that could activate latent desires to revitalize what is primary in their cultural identity: being stewards of their ancestral lands.

Other organizations on the Colorado Plateau are implementing programs and projects that will add to the coalition of connectors attempting to restore agriculture on the Colorado Plateau. They are too numerous to mention here, but the message is that an unrest is stirring that can lead only to resilient reactions and actions that will somehow keep people such as Eric coaxing foods from the dry, sandy soils of the Colorado Plateau.

Notes

1. Hopi Ogres are a class of katchina: spirits that return to the Hopi communities during ceremonies in their honor.

2. A Hopi creation story tells how the Creator offered the Hopi the choice of several types of corn. Their selection would foretell their future as a people.

They chose the smallest ear, signifying that their lives would be not only diffi-cult but also long and full of wisdom.

3. Kivas are the semi-underground structures that the Hopi and other Puebloan elders and ceremonial leaders periodically enter during ceremony and ritual.

4. A good reference for the archaeology of Chaco Canyon and other past civilizations in the Greater Southwest can be found in Stephan H. Lekson, ed., *The Archaeology of Chaco Canyon: An Eleventh-Century Pueblo Regional Center* (Santa Fe, NM: SAR Press, 2006).

5. Personal communication with Mark Varien, January 7, 2010.

6. The majority of Hopi still living on the Hopi reservation occupy villages on top of three mesas. All three mesas are elongated in geologic structure and rest on the dry Colorado Plateau landscape only a mile or two from each other. Beginning with the westernmost mesa, they are commonly referred to as the First, Second, and Third mesas.

7. The Natwani Coalition is a nonprofit organization that operates under its parent nonprofit organization, the Hopi Foundation.

5

Bounty among the Saguaro

SHE WAS STEPPING in my footprints. At first, I didn't realize what she was doing. I was trying not to stumble on the uneven, rocky Sonoran Desert soil as I wound my way around the creosote and brittle bushes, trying not to get my legs punctured by cholla cactus. I was leading a project director for an East Coast film crew through the desert near the Gila River south of Phoenix, Arizona. I was hired by the company to help preview a site where it was hoping to film a group of Native artists creating "on the spot art" in the Sonoran Desert. I glanced back to check on her when I noticed what she was doing. I stopped, smiled, and asked in a teasing way, "Why are you stepping in my steps?" I simultaneously held back a laugh and felt sympathy at her response. She admitted that she was deathly afraid of snakes and assumed that I, who was a Native person and desert dweller, knew where the snakes were and that I would be able to avoid any. By following my tracks, she was hoping that, by default, she would also avoid the snakes. There was probably some logic to her assumptions. I have been traversing desert lands on foot for nearly all my life. Is it possible that one develops a sort of anti-snake radar as a result of being among them for so long? Probably not, but it is possible to communicate in other ways with desert life that is neither scalable or measurable and that can lead today's desert dwelling descendants to maintain and revive patterns of resilient stewardship among the Saguaro.

Figure 5.1 Sonoran desert landscape; southwest of Tucson, Arizona.

Saguaro are an indicator species for the Sonoran Desert, a hot and arid region that stretches south from just north of Phoenix and all the way down into northwest Mexico to the state of Sinaloa. The Sonoran Desert ends to the east where it meets the Chihuahuan Desert just before the border of Arizona and New Mexico. Its western boundary meets the Colorado River and the Sea of Cortez, although some scholars and mapmakers include Baja, California, as part of the Sonoran Desert. Nevertheless, it is one of the largest desert regions in the world, covering nearly 120,000 square miles. Cold weather refugees from the northern climes, such as Alberta, Saskatchewan, the Dakotas, and Minnesota, often flock to the Sonoran Desert in their huge motor homes during the winter. In the summer, these "snow bunnies" pack up their lawn chairs and bird feeders and head back north. Except for those that live full time in the Sonoran Desert, the region is generally avoided during the summer. The average annual rainfall there is less than 10 inches, which arrives mostly in the winter months and during the annual monsoon season that begins in July. Temperatures reach up to 120 degrees during the hottest month of June.

The Sonoran Desert is home to about 60 species of mammals, 350 different bird species, and 20 species of amphibians, 100 plus reptile species, 30 native fish, and more than 2,000 native plants. The Sonoran Desert includes plants from the agave family, palm family, cactus family, and legume family, to name a few. The flora and fauna that thrive in the harsh conditions of the Sonoran Desert have evolved specialized adaptations to survive arid conditions. People coevolved with this desert as well. At the time of European contact, over 25 distinct indigenous cultures thrived in the Sonoran Desert. The desert is still the homeland for 14 Native cultures, including the Tohono O'odham, Akimel O'odham, Hia-Ced O'odham, Seri, Maricopa Apache, Tonto Apache, Yavapai, Mohave, Pima, Cocopah, Quechuan, Yaqui, Mayo, and Opata. When most people consider deserts, they think of vast, harsh, desolate places devoid of life. Therefore, few people realize that the Sonoran Desert offers a bounty of diversity stewarded for centuries by these 14 Native cultures.

Earlier, it was noted how Cabeza de Vaca commented about the bounty of the landscape when he and his lost companions stumbled their way into the Sonoran Desert region. Of special interest was where they noted several varieties of what they called *calabasas*, which were no doubt different kinds of locally raised squashes. They partook of the colorful mix of corn offered them by their Native hosts and enjoyed bowls of assorted beans. It is probable that, at one or more of the feasts Cabeza de Vaca attended while in the Sonoran Desert, he and his friends were served mesquite flour porridges and greens wild crafted from the landscape and from the edges of the agricultural fields. Cabeza de Vaca also noted in his journals the diversity of fruits that he had no name for, but still relished. I can imagine that prickly pear and other cacti fruits were served up as well as desert hackberry, capulin, the sweet heart of agave, and perhaps the bittersweet papache.

One of today's stewards of the Sonoran Desert's bounty is the Yaqui deer singer Felipe Molina. Felipe is not a farmer, although the Yaqui, also known as Yoeme, have tilled the Sonoran Desert for centuries. Felipe is an educator working in the school systems around Tucson, Arizona, primarily with Yaqui youth. Outside of the normal school system, he offers a form of education focused on singing other dimensions of reality into existence. Felipe is schooling young Yaqui in the art of deer singing.

The deer songs act as linguistic portals between this dimension and the one in which the Surem live. The Surem are residents of an historical/mystical space in which the Yaqui feel they used to reside. As a result of a community decision, they chose to leave the Huya Ania, the place where all Yaqui first lived, to enter this world. However, those Yaqui that chose not to leave this special place became the Surem. Today's Yaqui believe that the Surem can sometimes be seen in desert regions outside modern-day Yaqui communities. They resemble little people and can be found in desert trees and shrubs. When I consider the stories of the Surem, I can't help but envision thin, little dark-skinned people with huge eyes and mischievous toothy smiles fading in and out of reality much like Lewis Carroll's Cheshire cat. Yaqui deer songs are vehicles for expressing and understanding the history surrounding the Surem. They are performed throughout the year in specially erected ramadas the Yaqui refer to as *ramá*. Deer songs are still sung in the various Yaqui villages in Sonora, Mexico, and in the newer villages that were established after the Yaqui diaspora at the turn of the last century. There are usually one or three singers accompanied by flute, a brazilwood rasp, and a gourd water drum. The songs are fast and repetitive. It seems that the singers would have difficulty catching their breath in between verses, but somehow they endure the rapid staccato of the drum, rasp, and flute. The songs express notions of a space in an otherworldly time and dimension where everything is perfect and full of flowers. I was watching deer singers in the small Yaqui community of Guadalupe outside of Phoenix, Arizona, in the early 1990s. On that warm evening, we were surrounded by a night sky that faded out the stars due to light pollution from the nearby sprawling metropolis. The air was filled with thick, zesty smells of Mexican foods, the sound of screaming children, and the staccato of the musicians. I asked a woman why she was smiling during the deer songs. She said, "Songs take us back to where everything is perfect."

The deer songs are performed for the Surem and for the Sea Ania, the flower world that exists beneath the dawn. In this space, all is perfect, including Yaqui deer hunters. They stalk the deer and are in communication with this creature, which is an intermediary between one world and another. As an author, Felipe provided a symbolically rich narrative of Yoeme sacred space and ritual in his book, *Yaqui Deer Songs.* From Molina, we learn that Yoeme sacred space is a vivid, spiritually poetic human and natural dimension that is comprised of several components. The night world is called Tuka Ania; the dream world is called Tenku Ania; the flower world is called Sea Ania; and the enchanted world is called Yo Ania.

In the East, at the place beneath the dawn, exists the flower world, Sea Ania. This place is an idealistic, prototypical natural world filled with model insects, flowers, animals, including the deer, and all the natural components of the Sonoran Desert are mirrored in its perfected beauty. Deer songs celebrate, describe, and praise the flower world in order to maintain the important relationship with it. The deer dance and songs of *Mayo Maso* (deer dancers) are poetic expressions of their sacred "little brother" deer, who is closely associated with flowers and the dawn. The accompaniment of the gourd water drum and the brazilwood rasp form together an integral expression of the flower world and dawn.

Although deer singers, singers, and orators from Native groups are not always the individuals that till the soil, save seeds, and plant heirloom crops, their role is as crucial for resilience and the preservation of biocultural diversity. Their songs and oratory are expressed in a language that has given voice to their particular landscapes for centuries. Language is an audible expression of symbols. The symbols of language express meanings that are shared by the speakers of that language. Anthropologist Bronislaw Malinowski demonstrated an appreciation for the relationship between natural places and languages in his work on "garden words" among the Trobriand Islanders during the 1930s. Malinowski focused on the linguistic importance of magical words and their meaning. He stated that nature "assumes an exceptional place in the savage's view of the world," because it is the natural world that provides essentially all the "edible species of animals or plants." I am not sure I appreciate having myself and my relatives referred to as "savages," but Malinowski's point is similar to my earlier notion of kincentricity.

During the 1940s, linguist Benjamin Whorf reshaped Malinowski's notion of "exceptional place" into what he called a "stream of sensory experience." Among the series of articles he wrote, Whorf concluded that if language, culture, and thought are partially shaped by experiences, then it can be concluded that some of the experiences of a culture stem from its relationships with its natural environment. Whorf's conclusions would later be reexamined by a host of linguistic and cognitive researchers. They all suggest that language and cognition are embodied; that is, the mind is partly shaped by its external experiences with the environment. Embodiment can also be considered in a double sense; that which "encompasses both the body as a lived, experiential structure and the body as the context or milieu of cognitive mechanisms" (Varela, 1991). In *The Spell of the Sensuous*, David Abram states that "humans are tuned for relationships." If, as Abram suggests, humans are ingrained with a propensity to connect with the natural world, does it follow then that the natural world is only an inert mass of complex carbons and chemical compounds? Indigenous paradigms suggest the opposite, implying that the human–nature relationship requires both parties to participate in the dance of life; it takes two to tango.

Ethnobiological studies related to lexical development have assumed a human-centered imposed classification on nature. They suggest that taxonomies and lexicons, the categories that people conjure up, are a result of a human need to act upon and categorize an inanimate natural world. Most ethnoscientists assume that humans maintain a logical mind that will invariably find the natural structure in their environments as opposed to environments affecting the ordering scheme developed by humans. The result is that ethnobiological research has ignored sizable portions of the possibilities available today that may help science gain deeper insights into human–landscape relationship concerns. It must be understood that only a few ethnobiologists are also trained as anthropologists. A minority of this group concentrates on the semantic and cognitive aspects of ethnobiology.

When semantic and cognitive elements are looked at, another deeper realm of Native special–temporal reality begins to unfold. Among Uto-Aztecan speakers, which include Yaqui, Hopi, Mayo, and Rarámuri speakers, there are many references to flowers in most of the ceremonial and other songs and oratory. What becomes obvious is that flowers could be metaphors of a deeply ingrained relationship to the biodiversity of the regions within which the Uto-Aztecan speakers live. Another way to express this is that flower as well as plant-related metaphors are abundant linguistic expressions of nature. They are also found in cultural history and in names for plants and people. Mental spaces and metaphors draw structure and meaning from culturally cognized models and are essential aspects of cognitive studies. Some of the deeper insights into Native perceptions of land and plants were derived from metaphors.

Metaphors are important to the understanding of how land-based cultures are able to enhance diversity. Ecologically related metaphors pervade everyday language, which means they permeate thought and action. Metaphors are critical to interpreting daily realities of landscapes. One of the most lucrative places to search for metaphors is in language, because language is based on the same conceptual system used in actions and thought. Therefore, metaphors are central to normal daily discourse and reflect human understanding and experiences of the world.

When dealing with metaphors in Native cultures, it is important to be aware of hidden aspects that are inconsistent with the focus of the metaphor. Context becomes an essential aspect of metaphor analysis. Metaphors create mental images that can align discontinuities into cultural and contextual meaning. In other words, metaphors help humans to understand abstract concepts in concrete terms.

In general, metaphors offer glimpses into the most fundamental values of a culture. They unveil which values are important and offer a means of understanding cosmology, religion, and cultural concepts. It is important to understand that cultural words carry more contextual meaning than simply the objects that they denote. Cultural and social meanings are encoded in many terms for the land. When we name and label things, we afford them being-ness, adding them into encoded categories of experience unique to certain limited cultural contexts. When labels are used, they are dependent on the context in which they are spoken. Therefore, it is essential that ethnobiologists afford deeper consideration of metaphor in the analysis of plant names and classification. It is also important to recognize the contributions of ethnobiological studies that suggest, "There is a level of biological classification that corresponds to 'natural groupings' of organisms which possess 'bundles' of correlated features and which are 'obviously' different from other organisms." What all this suggests is that rigid, hierarchically ordered human classification is rare; and categorization develops within a culture at a certain point in time in order to best gain maximum information of an event or thing with the least cognitive effort.

All this linguistic and cognitive exercise has been a way of suggesting that Native languages are reflections of the landscapes within which they developed and that the speakers of those languages use their languages as mediums through which they express their relationships to their places. As a result, it is little wonder that there is a close correlation between the loss of languages around the world and the loss of biodiversity. Currently, there are over 5,000 languages spoken worldwide, and this diversity of languages is spoken by mostly indigenous speakers. Another way to look at it is that about 96 percent of the world's languages are spoken by about 3 percent of the world's peoples, and most of them are indigenous peoples. Unfortunately, fewer than 10,000 people speak over half of the world's languages. By the end of the twenty-first century, the world's symphony of languages will become more like a quartet when the human legacy of cultural diversity is reduced to about 10 percent of what it currently is. Disappearing with those languages will be the unique and landscape-specific traditional ecological knowledge, innovations, practices, and paradigms.

According to the fourteenth edition of *Ethnologue*, about 32 percent of existing Native languages survive in Asia, followed by 30 percent on the African continent, 19 percent in the Pacific, and then 15 percent in North America. The highest concentration of indigenous languages is found in Papua New Guinea, where about 850 languages are still spoken on an island no larger in land mass than the state of Texas. Such concentrations of indigenous languages can be considered linguistic hot spots. Conservation International uses the notion of "hot spots" to highlight locations around the world where biodiversity is not only highest but also at risk of being lost due to extractive industry, over harvesting of natural resources, cattle ranches, pollution, and other human threats. The other hot spots include Southeast Asia, Western Africa, the

Pacific Islands, and the Americas, especially in Mexico and Brazil. Many of these surviving languages are considered "nearly extinct" by linguists that keep track of these figures. The current number of nearly extinct languages is between 6 and 11 percent. This means that these languages are spoken by only a handful of elders and that the next generations are not learning the languages. In the Americas, which include North, Central, and South America, about 161 languages are considered nearly extinct. Many more are considered endangered or have already disappeared.

For the longest time, the conservation and environmental movement had assumed that the human–environment equation would always result negatively for the land. The last couple of hundred years of exponential human population growth coupled with mass expansions of industry and globalization have certainly done little to balance out the equation. As a result, until recently, researchers had not considered the possibility that humans could actually enhance their landscapes; that human communities might actually play a role in increasing diversity; or that humans could be a keystone species of some ecological systems. The Great Yellowstone Fire of 1988 played a catalyzing role in waking up conservationists to the once taboo concept of allowing wildfires to continue unabated. After the fire, historical studies emerged, showing that forest fuel levels reflected in the amount of understory and relative thickness of new and old tree growth were at their highest in recent decades. Land managers began to question what, in the past, had allowed for conditions in which fuel levels were lower, thereby creating conditions for less intense fires that were not as catastrophic as the ones burning today. The answers that slowly emerged all pointed to pre-Columbian human manipulation of the landscapes.

Wherever people have been in sustainable contact with and cultivation of a landscape, there has emerged a culturally recognized and sanctioned pattern of using and talking about that environment. It should not be surprising then to notice, residing in the most biodiverse regions of the world, certain human communities that continue their cultural legacies reflected first in the survival of their language.

Humans tend to think in their first language. There are a few lucky people that are able to both dream and think in several languages. Nevertheless, language is thought, and a reflection of action and practices. Encoded in Native languages are ecological patterns of behaving with landscapes. Back in the 1990s, when I had been trying to learn more about deer singing and deer songs, Felipe Molina invited me to his home in Marana, Arizona. Marana is located about 20 miles west of Tucson among quickly disappearing agricultural fields. The farms are being replaced by the Tucson region's urban sprawl. Marana is one of the three original Yaqui diaspora communities that emerged over 100 years ago. Today, it is a small neighborhood of low-slung cinder-block houses situated among dusty streets. Small flower and vegetable doorway and yard gardens give additional color to the yellows and pinks that people have painted the exterior of their homes. Felipe met me outside in the shade of a Palo Verde tree; we talked and then went for a walk. Our walk led us past the rows of nearby fields and then the unmarked boundary that separates the community from the open desert. As we walked, I noticed that Felipe was holding his hands low toward the spiny Sonoran Desert plants while sometimes lightly touching them. He noticed my attention to his hands and said that this was how he communicated with the land and was able to receive new deer songs.

Deer singing, it turns out, is more than simply memorizing lyrics to a set of songs; it is an entire way of living, being, and communicating with one's universe. Deer songs are more like conversations between the singer, the deer, and the wilderness world. The deer singer must maintain a constant connection with the deer and the wilderness world in order to be able to sing the songs properly. The songs are recounted throughout the year with new ones being "composed" nearly all the time. The songs are not written down, but are passed on through the generations of deer singers. To write down the songs would be similar to bringing them to a sort of textual death, which would then bring death to the wilderness world.

Written texts transform nature into silent and static symbols void of being-ness and vitality. When written texts become substitutes for nature, the nature ceases to breathe and loses its color and dynamic, un-resting personality. I enjoy nature writing and recognize its value for those who rarely or never have the opportunity to experience wildness firsthand. My point, however, is that each essay, story, and description is only a snapshot of nature at any given moment. We can pick and choose the moments that we wish to experience. For Native people, however, nature is not momentary nor is it outside ourselves; we breathe with it. When Felipe sings deer songs, he is voicing this living and mutually life-giving relationship. The songs renew the life of the wilderness world each time they are composed and recited.

Many modern Yaqui spend little time in the wilderness. Economic disparities on both sides of the US–Mexico border have created harsh realities whereby people must work long hours for little compensation. Another fact of life is that the villages north of the border are in urban settings with little opportunity for wilderness experiences. Therefore, another job of the deer singers and dancers is to periodically sing the Huya Ania and Sea Ania to life during ceremonies. For each deer dance, a ramada is constructed. During that period when the singers and dancers are present, the ramada becomes the wilderness world. The space housed within the ramada becomes sacred, much like an ephemeral portal into another dimension of reality and sacredness. Another way to consider this phenomenon is that the Yaqui people carry with them their sacred space and release their cargo in a sort of shared group consciousness, lifting what was at one moment dry soil, mesquite posts, stone, and branches into a reality of sacredness. The deer singers are catalysts for creating a new sacred homeland that each dances. Not far away, another community of people that have long dwelled in the Sonoran Desert has been working tirelessly to revitalize its relationship to its homeland.

Imagine growing up in a community in which a child knows that over half of the adults in his family, the adults that he sees at the grocery store, and those that he comes in contact with at other times, will all die from the same disease. To add to the effect of the psychological trauma of this understanding, is also the realization that the child has a 60 percent chance of dying from that disease. Terrol Dew Johnson and Tristan Reader, codirectors of Tohono O'odham Community Action (TOCA), live with this reality every day on the Tohono O'odham reservation in southern Arizona. They are working tirelessly to change this reality for the next generation of O'odham (Desert People). In the United States, the loss of traditional diets has been under way for several generations. The most profound changes occur among the young who are raised in a Big Gulp nutritional culture. A significant portion of the daily diet for Native people, for example, includes fried processed foods, fast food meals, and soda pops, all low in fiber and complex carbohydrates and high in fat. Despite romanticized opinions, most Native people today do not eat the foods eaten by their ancestors over 100 years ago. This is an unfortunate fact because those foods could serve as lifesavers for the thousands of Native people now suffering and dying from adult-onset type 2 diabetes.

Traditional foods are slow to digest. Foods such as prickly pear, mesquite, beans, flour corn, wild greens and berries, wild tubers, acorns, and wild grains are all high in soluble and insoluble fibers and mucilages, which act to prevent the body from quickly digesting the complex carbohydrates and turning them into sugars. In addition, many of these foods contain a starch called amylose, which digests slowly, resulting in the slow release of glucose and insulin. Starches found in modern foods such as white bread and potatoes break down quickly and precipitate sharp and high levels of sugars in the blood, which can spark diabetes. A study done for The American Society for Clinical Nutrition tested the in vivo glycemic index of traditional foods (an index that reveals the speed at which certain foods cause the release of glucose and insulin). The test demonstrated that flour corn, mesquite pods, tepary beans (beans hybridized by Tohono O'odham ancestors), and acorns were all low in glycemic response and insulin release, ranging from 16 for acorns to 40 for flour corn. The glycemic index for canned sweet corn is around 59, whereas those of other modern foods are much higher. The study demonstrated the importance of not only traditional foods but also foods high in fiber and those that contain slow-digesting starches.

The benefits of an indigenous traditional diet are numerous. The diet not only offers fuel for high endurance but also provides the ingredients necessary for the prevention of food-related illnesses and disease. It is the pharmacological effects of traditional foods that offer these health benefits. People who are prone to or who already suffer from type 2 diabetes need to regulate their glucose and insulin levels. However, when the modern diet, which contains little fiber and large quantities of simple carbohydrates, is consumed, it is digested and readily broken down by the body, which results in the quick release of glucose and insulin. Fat accumulates along with a rise in blood sugar. As this continues over the years, it can result in type 2 diabetes. The traditional diet is high in fiber and complex carbohydrates; is low in fat and cholesterol; and offers the full range of minerals, vitamins, and proteins required for human health. The soluble and insoluble fibers, complex carbohydrates, and mucilages help to control glucose and insulin levels, help people to lose weight, and lower cholesterol levels. As a result, the occurrence of diabetes, obesity, and heart disease is very low among the indigenous populations in northwest Mexico that still maintain a traditional diet. Cancer and ulcers are virtually unheard of for people who subsist primarily on traditional foods.

Another health problem that strikes indigenous people who turn to a modern diet is weight gain. Obesity is closely associated with diabetes and other health problems. The consumption of high-fiber traditional foods prevents obesity. High-fiber foods are low in fat and slow to digest, which also controls the appetite. High fiber lowers serum insulin, which also decreases food intake because insulin stimulates hunger.

In addition to the benefits of reducing and preventing obesity, a high-fiber traditional diet prevents high blood pressure and serum cholesterol. Several studies have demonstrated the blood pressure–reducing effects of a high-fiber diet. In all the studies, subjects who consumed a vegetarian high-fiber diet had significant reduction in blood pressure.[1] An important side effect of the traditional diet is the lowering of serum cholesterol, a contributor to vascular and heart disease, and strokes. Traditional foods contain gums, pectins, and psyllium, which all control and lower cholesterol levels in the body.

Beans are an especially important part of the traditional diet. Leguminous fibers found in beans have a special effect on postprandial glucose levels: glucose levels that result after a meal. It is the sudden rise in postprandial glucose levels that affects diabetes. After meals, glucose levels generally rise due to the digestion of carbohydrates and starches, which are transformed into sugars. Eating lots of fiber in a meal can control postprandial levels, but leguminous fibers seem to control these levels without having to stuff oneself with other fibers. The mucilaginous bean coats slow down the digestion process. Beans are also high in proteins and complex carbohydrates, which adds nutritionally to their already beneficial fiber. The additional benefit of eating unprocessed foods such as beans, seeds, and whole grains is the trace of chromium found in their hulls and seed coats. Chromium deficiency has been found to cause insulin resistance. When foods are processed, the chromium in the seed coats and hulls literally goes down the drain. Traditional food processing generally does not remove the seed coats and hulls from foods; therefore, the chromium stays in the meal.

In many ways foods reflect culture. The stories, taboos, ceremonies, and human interactions that surround food are portholes into the myriad of fascinating ways in which people relate to their diet, to their natural environment, and to each other. Nutrition is secondary to the culturally contrived manners that people adhere to: control food production, procurement, when to eat certain foods, how to prepare them, and what they should or will eat. Today, the nutritional benefits of indigenous foods are highlighted in clinical studies and in the pages of health magazines. The nutritional aspects of the foods have risen to a more important level than the social ones. We often neglect the social, the people and their cultural models, and their mental states when we clinically study foods.

One study conducted by David Kozak during the early 1990s demonstrated that many Pima psychologically "surrendered" to diabetes. It was so prevalent in their community that they assumed that they would die from the disease and did little to mitigate its effects, even though they were exposed to information about how to prevent the disease. Johnson and Reader of TOCA plan to mitigate the effects of poor nutrition with a long-term strategy of traditional farming, food access, exercise, and education. The key to their approach is to introduce their programming within culturally familiar and acceptable boundaries. The educational element of their program is brought to the O'odham youth by means of storytelling and through art programs that invite children to research and share what they are learning about foods through painting, pottery, and other artistic media. The beauty is that the storytelling and art projects invite the children's parents and elders to participate in bridging the generational linguistic gap. The importance of exercise is emphasized through games long played by the O'odham; one such game resembles a form of desert-style full-contact field hockey. Food access is a difficult facet of TOCA's programming. As mentioned, the Big Gulp diet permeates O'odham daily existence. People's contemporary Native–Rez identities are partially constructed around access to highly processed and fast foods. Unfortunately, these foods are now most readily available on the Tohono O'odham and other Native reservation communities. TOCA's response is to bring traditional foods such as tepary beans, cholla buds, corn, squashes, cactus fruit teas, and other desert foods directly to the people's mouths through school lunch and elderly care programs. TOCA pulled a huge coup in 2003 when it got the only local grocery chain represented on the reservation to begin carrying TOCA's brand of traditional foods.

The key element to TOCA's program is that it raises and wild crafts all the foods it sells, cooks, and educates the public about.

The drive to Sells, Arizona, where TOCA is located, takes you mostly along a two-lane highway through a typical Sonoran Desert landscape marked by centuries-old tall and columnar saguaro cactus, spiny olive-green creosote bushes, yellow-flowered brittlebush, barrel cactus, Palo Verde trees, and mesquite trees. On most days, one can cast the eye across a desert view that stretches 50 miles. About 15 miles south and west of Tucson, I like to stop at a dusty turnout on the side of the highway and absorb the desert outside the confines of the air-conditioned car. My thoughts begin to ride the warm currents that swirl among and around the spiny desert flora. Among my senses that are usually greeted by the Sonoran Desert, is my ability to smell the assertive scent of creosote, which is normally the first to present itself. After creosote introduces itself to me, the next members of the Sonoran Desert party show up. They include the heat, the brightness of the atmosphere, and then the desert buzz, which is at first nearly imperceptible, but grows in magnitude as one's ears begin to filter out everything else. I have never asked any desert biologist or ecologist what this buzz could be. But I am guessing that it is a symphony composed of the fusion of sounds such as the buzz of billions of insects; the stretching and unfolding of all the desert plants; the scratching of trillions and trillions of cactus spines; the wind sunning itself on desert rocks, cliffs, and plants; and all this life searching for one more drop of moisture. The Sonoran Desert is the most diverse desert on the planet, hosting over 400 useful plants. If one maintains an intimate relationship with this place, it is not too difficult to survive here. The O'odham have accomplished this partly by hybridizing domesticated crops to this arid and hot region.

TOCA's grow out farm takes advantage of a slight natural angle to the several acres that sit at the mouth of a shallow wash. When it rains, the water flows down the wash at a relatively slow pace and into the farmland. O'odham agriculturalists have utilized this technique for centuries. For a couple of hundred years, the O'odham tried their hand at irrigation. This was during their attempt to build and maintain a trading civilization, which archaeologists refer to as the Hohokam period, circa AD 950–1500. Researchers borrowed the word *Hohokam* from the Pima language. It means "those who have gone," or "those who have vanished." Archaeologist Emil Haury, who has studied the Hohokam, provided a more literal translation of "all used up." For a while, the Hohokam civilization maintained an incredible array of agricultural fields located around what today is the Phoenix basin, watered by the Salt and Gila rivers. When the project director that was mentioned at the beginning of this chapter was matching my footsteps, we were walking through one of the most populated and complex communities during the eleventh century, which is referred to today as Snaketown. The only thing left of Snaketown now is some mounds reburied by early archaeologists. At one time, canals emanated from the two rivers and irrigated vast fields of desert crops. The canal system became a web of moist life for the inhabitants that probably numbered around 1,000 people during its height. It is speculated that the flood-style irrigation practiced by the Hohokam eventually caused over salinization of the desert soils, which over time reduced the productivity of the fields. This coupled with rapid growth and a long drought placed too much stress on the system, which eventually collapsed. The final blow may ironically have been too much rain. It is an interesting example of historical irony that the City of Phoenix is also watered by canals that bring water from the Colorado River into the modern basin. The current canals rest exactly on top of the web of ancient Hohokam canals and carry water to a thirsty city experiencing rapid growth and trying to survive an ongoing drought.

According to retired archaeologist Jim Judge, the Hohokam canal system was ill prepared for silt. Jim conducted a series of dendrochronological (tree-ring) studies of trees that were growing at the headwaters of the Salt and Gila rivers during the Hohokam late classic period (AD 1125). According to the tree rings, there was a period of heavy rains that would have sent extra silt down the rivers and into the Hohokam canals. The Hohokam had devised a system of small dams as a way to control the waters flowing into and through their ditches. The silt-laden flows came downhill and into the canals. Soon, the dams were challenged and began to give way as a result of the buildup. In other words, there was too much water, and soon their fields were inundated and abandoned.

Today's O'odham are the descendants of the canal builders. Their current system is less dependent on canals and dams and more attuned to the natural flows of the seasons and elements. Ingenious O'odham farmers have developed crops especially suited to high heat and little rain. They grow a corn that can mature in 60 days with little moisture. White and brown tepary beans grow better and produce more bean pods with little rain. If they receive too much rain, the plants actually produce mostly leaves and very few pods. O'odham squashes and melons grow at the end of elongated vines and are juicy. O'odham agriculture and their traditional foodways are uniquely connected not only to what the people can grow but also to what they can cultivate from their very large garden, that is, the Sonoran Desert. Throughout the year, the people can collect the plentiful and sweet mesquite pods that fall from the low-slung trees. Mesquite trees, like other fruit-bearing species, are subject to competition for moisture. When the understory of creosote, encelia, and other desert flora becomes too plentiful in the shade of the trees, the mesquite trees reduce their production of pods in order to save their precious moisture and glucose for the leaves and trunk of the tree. Early O'odham collectors no doubt observed this phenomenon and made efforts periodically to clear the understory from their favorite collection sites. Cholla buds that grow like small yellow acorn squash at the ends of the spiny cactus limbs are collected early in the year along with edible greens. Both come forth after winter rains that saturate the desert. During the early spring, it seems that the desert just can't hold back its enthusiasm and lets go with a huge "sight-gasm" of colors in the form of flowers. Soon after, the flowering plants transform to their edible version that the people take advantage of. Afterward, the cholla and greens are ready, and the cacti spring forth with sweetened versions of the cholla in the form of prickly pear and saguaro fruit. Finally, chia plants are ready to be harvested of their tiny, but nutritious, loads of grains at the same time that the O'odham early crops are ready. It is as though early after the Hohokam experiment collapsed, the scattered O'odham devised the perfect conspiracy by timing the planting of their crops, the wild crafting of desert foods, and the final harvesting with the desert seasons, thereby keeping efforts to maintain the human–landscape cycles to a comfortable minimum.

Note

1. For diet and diabetes studies, see Anderson, James W. "Dietary Fiber and Human Health." *HortScience 25* (12, 1990): 1488. Also, Simpson, H.C.R., S. Lousley, M. Greekie, R.W. Simpson, R.D. Carter, T.D.R. Hockaday, and J.I. Mann. "A High Carbohydrate Leguminous Fibre Diet Improves all Aspects of Diabetic Control," *The Lancet 1* (1981):1.

6

Small Fields for Large Impacts on the Colorado Plateau

"THERE'S NOTHING OUT there," she said. One of my students from the East Coast was leaning her head against the warm window of the fifteen-passenger van as we traversed the Navajo reservation in northern Arizona. She also wondered out loud how anyone could survive in this place. I believe that she was equally concerned about how she and her fellow students would survive should the group experience some misfortune. From most vantage points, the Colorado Plateau appears dry and desolate, and we were on our way to spend two weeks in the field camping for an Ethnobotany Field School.

At first glance, the student's concern and wonder seemed appropriate. The landscape appears very much like the scenes of desolate landscape marked by sandstone cliffs showcased in innumerable Hollywood movies and in nature programs. However, unlike the fantasies encouraged by Hollywood, the Colorado Plateau of northern Arizona, the southernmost segment of Utah, the southwest corner of Colorado, and the northwest portion of New Mexico house an incredible array of biocultural diversity stewarded today by resilient Native farmers, young Native activists, and dedicated individuals that think of this place as home.

Figure 6.1 Navajo cornfield on an Ancestral Puebloan agricultural site; north of Winslow, Arizona.

On the surface of things, water is as scarce as the vegetation, although huge aquifers lie underneath most of the Plateau. During normal years, the land receives less than 10 inches of precipitation annually; and this comes in a bimodal pattern, meaning it comes in torrents during the summer monsoon season when washes temporarily become rivers and once dusty and washboarded roads transform into red-brown mud bogs. The other rainy period is during the winter when the female rain comes, as Navajo people refer to it, softly touching the thirsty land. Today, due to climate shifts, the Plateau is even drier. Somehow, despite the aridity, peoples have flourished and continue to flourish on this landscape. Over 10,000 years ago, Paleo-Indians, as anthropologists call these early ancestors, began to hunt, camp, and gather in the area. They camped around springs and followed the few watercourses, leaving their mark as chiseled and painted art on cliffs and large boulders. Later, beginning about 8,000 years ago, some people began to cultivate crops and were settling on the land, again in locations where water was present. By the time the first Spanish conquistadores were scouting the region for possible gold in 1540, the Colorado Plateau had become a cultural and linguistic hot spot. Seven linguistic families were represented on the Plateau. Among these families, ten distinct languages are spoken, including Hopi, Navajo, Pai, Southern Paiute, Zuni, Keresan, Tewa, Towa, Apache, and Ute. The region has significance for linguistic diversity as well as being a beacon for American Indian linguistic survival. There remain approximately 361,978 speakers of Native languages in the United States, and 51 percent of these speakers speak languages unique to the Colorado Plateau. The Plateau is also home to numerous plant and animal species, some of which are endemic only to the region.

The current landscape differs from what it was when early Spanish explorers described grasses high enough to tickle the bellies of their horses. When one reads early accounts written by explorers such as those in the scouting parties of Coronado or the exploring expeditions of John Wesley Powell and James Ohio Pattie, one feels that these men experienced the land much like the ancestors of today's indigenous inhabitants did. They felt the land with their noses to the ground and recognized the abundance that can seem to be hidden. The late writer and activist Edward Abbey once suggested that the only way for a person to really experience the land is to move about it on hands and knees, getting it in one's nostrils, under one's fingernails, and in one's food.

My students and I managed to experience the Colorado Plateau much as Abbey suggested. After two weeks of camping on the sandy red soils, getting it in their food and in their eyes, and crushing sagebrush leaves between their fingers in order to inhale the pungent scent, the students were sad that the trip was over. There exist a diversity of biota and a heterogeneity on the Plateau that cannot be seen through a van window. Such can be experienced only by walking across a Hopi mesa where fissures on the tabletop reveal microclimates of lichen, flowers, and herbs fed by the tiniest rivulets of water. Or it can be found when one climbs the 8 miles from the Havasupai community of Supai to the rim of the Grand Canyon. Along the way, the eye adjusts to the changes in hues of the soil while the ear listens first for the descending whistle of the Canyon Wren, and then by the time the rim is reached, the song shifts to the screech of the Piñon Jay. Another opportunity is for

the adventurous hiker to descend into the northern portion of Syc-
amore Canyon. In little time, the musky scents of pine forests that
wrap around a person like a welcoming blanket shrink away and are
replaced by tangy sweet smells of sumac. By the time the canyon
bottom is reached, the air is filled with a lofty veil similar to the moments prior to when the clouds are about to release their precious
moisture onto the dry land.

Native farmers pray and dance for life to sprout from the dry
soils of the Colorado Plateau. It was not only the individual farmers
whose fields introduced seasonal green mosaics to the reddish hues
of the Plateau; the agriculturalists were and remain supported by
weaves of community and spiritual relationships that reach deeper
than the thirstiest juniper roots. These collaborations between
human community, the land, the rain, and the skies developed after
significant commitments to make each other's conditions for life
the same. Resilient communities on the Colorado Plateau emerged
only after they became interdependent and interrelated with each
other and with their surroundings. These types of communities are
inclusive, reaching toward all the diversity that they share. They
shared a willingness to coexist with nature much like that of a marriage between people that requires a stick-to-itiveness in order for
the bond to be lasting. The bonds that have held the Hopi, Navajo,
Zuni, Pai, Apache, and Paiute to this land gained strength only
over long stretches of time. During recent times, however, those
bonds have been weakened, leading some to seek innovative mea-
sures for maintaining their connections to land and culture. Many
at the forefront of this battle have been the elderly. They are the
segments of traditional communities that maintain the cultural
memories central for short-term innovation to base its foundation
of innovative change and cultural revitalization.

In the past, small green fields dotted the landscape throughout
the Plateau. The people's reverence for the foods that people grow
is embedded in the origin stories and in holy plants. Farmers still
coax the holy corn, beans, and squash from the red soils of the
Colorado Plateau. Like other Native traditions, however, farming
suffers from lack of youth involvement and lack of a market. Also,
fewer and fewer people are eating the traditionally raised foods anymore. Convenience and access to fast and store-bought foods re-

duce the reliance on locally grown produce. In addition, lack of up-to-date information regarding food and nutrition places the Native consumer in a position of ignorance regarding what fast foods are doing to them.

Much effort is going into keeping traditional farming alive. These small fields will have large impacts on the Colorado Plateau. A key element in resilience thinking includes the concept that changes in ecosystems or, in the case of Native farmers, in societies take place in episodes interspersed with periods when "natural capital" builds up. Suddenly, these periods are flavored with what are called "reorganizations" of social "legacies," and this episodic behavior is caused by "interactions between fast and slow variables." On the Colorado Plateau, the natural capital is the farmers, the neighbors that lend a hand, the participating Native youth, and the wise elders. Several organizations are involved in reorganizing and developing new methods that can be used to revitalize and keep traditional agriculture alive in the region. The social legacy and the fast and slow variables that are interacting are the Native knowledge of how to coax food from the Plateau combined with the youth that will, no doubt, develop new ways to do this based on centuries-old traditions.

An old Navajo woman was seated in a metal folding chair. She was dressed in what has become traditional Navajo women's clothing: purple and green velvet and satin accentuated with a large silver and turquoise belt. Her neck, ears, fingers, wrist, and hair were also adorned with silver and turquoise. Her skin was dark and accented with lines and wrinkles that revealed a life spent outside on the Colorado Plateau. She looked at me as I entered the room and said with an accented and cynical voice, "Is this the big man that we have been waiting for?" After a pause for affect, she continued, "He's not so big." The other Navajo of various ages laughed quietly and began to fidget as I found a place to sit. I was about an hour late for this scheduled meeting with Developing Innovations in Navajo Education (DINE, Inc.), a partnership of Navajo farmers scattered across the wide expanses of the southwestern part of the Navajo reservation. We were in a cinder-block house transformed into a meeting place for the coalition located at Dilkon, Arizona. Kyril Calsoyas had agreed to meet me at a junction point near Dilkon. I came north from Interstate 40 somewhere between St. John's and Winslow, Arizona. I waited among the short, solitary greasewood bushes and sparse juniper watching turkey vultures circle overhead. The sky was that deep royal blue that seemed to appear even deeper blue in contrast to the reddish buttes, ridges, and hills unique to northern Arizona. After about 45 minutes of waiting, Kyril finally arrived in his small SUV that stirred up reddish dust when he pulled in next to me.

Kyril is not Navajo. He is one of many newcomers to the region, who, in most cases, come to escape the fast pace and stresses of city life. Kyril came at first for similar reasons, but has since dedicated his life to help revitalize sustainable Navajo agriculture on the reservation. The Navajo were never intensive agriculturalists like their Hopi and Zuni neighbors. Farming was mostly a backup system for gathering and hunting before European contact and for sheep pastoralism afterward. Still, their small fields dotted the landscape throughout Dinetah, the name of their traditional homeland. In addition, the Navajo reverence for corn is embedded in their origins. They also feel that they have traversed previous worlds in order to reach this fourth one. On the way, the ancestors became acquainted with and adopted four holy plants: tobacco, beans, squash, and corn.

The Navajo maintain a complex series of healing ceremonies often referred to as Chant Ways, Sings, and Beauty Ways. The ceremonies are intended to restore harmony to the patient or, as the Navajos say, hózhó. Some of the ceremonies, such as the Blessing Way, can last as long as 9 days and nights, during which the entire traditional history of the people is retold. In this way, both the Navajo world and the patient are revitalized and restored in harmony with their surroundings. An essential ingredient during these ceremonies is sand painting. A Singer (medicine man) directs the making of a sand painting that illustrates an allegoric tale used in the ceremony. After this, the painting must be ceremoniously destroyed before dawn, or else the Singer or the patient runs the risk of terrible spiritual reprisals.

In one ceremony, a sand painting called the Whirling Logs, or Tsil-ol-ne, is created. In this story, the hero sets out on a journey. During the journey, certain Navajo deities try to persuade him against going, but seeing his determination, help him hollow out a log in which he will travel down the river. Along the way, he experiences several events that result in his gaining important ceremonial knowledge. At one point, he is captured by the Water People, who force him beneath the waters to the home of Water Monster; but the hero is released after Black God threatens to burn down the house of Water Monster. During this event, Frog teaches the hero how to cure the illnesses caused by the Water People. When the hero finally reaches a big river, which is his destination, the deities take his log out of a whirlpool where the rivers meet and help him to shore.

The sand painting that accompanies this song depicts two deities: B'ganaskiddy (Talking God), the teacher, and Hastye-o-gahn (Calling God). They are shown in the painting as associated with farming and fertility. To the left and right of the deities are two humpbacked guardians. The humps on the figures are said to actually be backpacks, and the guardians are regarded as seed gatherers and bearers. The two guardians usually carry tobacco pouches. In the story, the hero comes upon a whirling cross where two Yeis, or spirit beings, and two pairs of males and females are seated on the four ends. From them, the hero gains the knowledge of farming and is given seeds. After this, he returns home and shares these gifts with the people. In the sand painting, these plants are shown as corn, beans, squash, and tobacco. The plants are also depicted as connected to the four sacred colors—white, blue, yellow, and black—and in their cardinal positions. These plants are depicted in the Father Sky and Mother Earth Narrative, which appears in many of the sand paintings throughout most of the Navajo healing ceremonies, including the Shooting Way, Mountain Way, and Blessing Way. They are called upon not because of a part in a particular story, but because of their strength and all-pervading importance. In the body of Mother Earth are the four sacred plants: corn, bean, squash, and tobacco.

After being appropriately put in my place by the old Navajo woman and after a couple more laughs at my expense, we sat down to a meeting to discuss the state of DINE, Inc.'s projects on that part of the reservation. Navajo farming has never died out. Farmers still coax the holy corn, beans, and squash from the red soils of the

Colorado Plateau. Like other Native traditions, however, Navajo farming suffers from lack of youth involvement and lack of market. A part of the DINE, Inc. plan is to identify markets for Navajo produce. Fewer and fewer Navajo are eating the traditionally raised foods anymore. Lack of convenient grocery stores and increasing access to fast food and store-bought foods reduce their reliance on locally grown produce. Also, lack of up-to-date information regarding food and nutrition places the Navajo consumers in a position of ignorance regarding what fast foods are doing to them. Kyril and his associates are hoping to educate the next generation of both Navajo consumers and farmers. But, first they needed a truck, a trailer, and a tractor.

The small Navajo agricultural fields are spread out over open expanses of sandy, dry, and rocky landscape. It has been noted that a huge aquifer lies below the surface of this region, but it is deep and rarely reaches the surface. Where it does, it consists of small springs that support endemic species of aquatic and plant life. Most of the springs do not flow to any usable degree. Navajo farmers, therefore, have taken advantage of areas on the landscape that are just depressed enough to collect rainwater. Rains naturally run to and remain just below the surface of these natural and temporary cisterns, which act like sponges, holding on to the precious moisture. At the edges of these locations grow species of plants found nowhere else. Frogs lay dormant in the soil, waiting for the next rainfall in order to take advantage of their dry respite so that they can once again croak a few bars to attract a mate, and then return to the soil once again. Some of these locations were used for agriculture by ancient Puebloan farmers and remain in use today by their Navajo tenants. A problem with these fields is they are spread out on the landscape in often difficult-to-reach places. A Navajo farmer may know of a farming neighbor whose fields are only 10 miles away, but due to deep arroyos and rocky terrain it may take over an hour to reach that neighbor by truck.

I visited one of these ancient, but still used, fields one fall after the harvest. The drying old cornstalks stood erect against the hot October sun. Their long leaves were parched and reached down toward the earth as though they were attempting to connect with the aquifer that they intuitively knew rested below the surface. The field was only about a half acre. It sat next to a sandy dirt road that attempted to suck the tires of our vehicles below the surface as we crept toward the field. Although from a distance the land on the Colorado Plateau that is not occupied by buttes, hills, or arroyos appears flat, most of it sits at an angle. The ingenuity of this ancient field was obvious when one stood at its edge. The southwest corner was probably several inches below the level of its northeast corner. Any rainwater that fell here would collect in the spongy soil and then creep downhill, feeding all the sown crops along the way. There was no mulch or waffle-shaped structures on this field. Navajo farming techniques here seemed to be direct: plant, pray and dance for rain, weed, and then harvest. The seed planted and saved for centuries seemed to instinctively know how to survive in this soil. But dry land farming is difficult and consumes lots of time.

Kyril noted that nearly all Navajo farmers hold day jobs. They don't have time to devote to their fields. In order to meet these needs, DINE, Inc. purchased a truck, a trailer, and a tractor that sits on that trailer. Justin Willy, a farmer himself, had been hired to traverse the reservation in this rig to help other farmers plow and till their fields. Laughter colors Justin's voice when he talks about having to drive 50 miles to plow a field, then turn around and drive the same 50 miles to plow another. This has become his job, which eats up time from his own fields. In order to contact Justin and to stay in touch with others, Kyril found help from a computer company. The company donated laptop computers so that the participating farmers can be online to check their messages, share weather and growing information, and check agricultural forecasts. The only glitch in this program is most Navajo farmers do have some electricity in their remote homes, but no satellite or cable hookups. In order to fire up their computers on cyberspace, they must drive and park near enough to one of the scores of Chapter Houses located throughout the reservation. Each Chapter House has installed a wireless computer network. Unless the farmers are going inside for a political meeting or to perhaps have a meal that some of the Chapter Houses serve to elders, they sit outside in the cab of their pickups, checking their e-mail. Justin said it sure beats having to drive 50 miles just to ask the next farmer over there if you can borrow his tiller.

Much effort is going into keeping Navajo farming alive. These small fields will have a large impact on the Colorado Plateau's ecological and social resilience. A key element in resilience thinking mentioned earlier in Chapter 4 includes the concept that changes in ecosystems or in human societies, like that of Navajo farmers, take place in periodic episodes when "natural capital" builds up. During these periods, "reorganizations" of social legacies catalyze the interactions between fast and slow variables. On the Navajo reservation, the natural capital is the farmers and people like Kyril, Justin, Hank, the participating Navajo youth, and the old woman. DINE, Inc. is involved in reorganizing and developing new methods to revitalize and keep traditional agriculture alive in the region. The social legacy and the fast and slow variables that are interacting are the Navajo knowledge of how to coax food from the Plateau combined with the youth, who will, no doubt, develop new ways to do this based on centuries-old traditions. On the Colorado Plateau, traditions are an asset and remain alive, especially when there is water available.

My Hopi friend Eric and I had another adventure in the Colorado Plateau. We were at the mouth of a canyon where we thought his huge Ford F250 was stuck in the sand. Jane had warned us to "be careful out there." We were trying to reach an agricultural area located north of Tuba City, Arizona. At that moment, I was beginning to question Eric's memory of the location of this place. The big tires of the truck spun deeper into the sand, exposing the moist layer beginning about 12 inches into the soil. It was hot out there. We were totally exposed. The ever-present turkey vultures located us and began to carve circles in the bluish-white sky above. After a few pushes, shoves, grunts, and strategically placed shovels, we were moving again. The truck headed toward what appeared to be a wall of red sandstone. Toward the left end of the wall, there appeared an opening. The sandy trail, passing for a road, directed us toward the opening. We rounded a corner into a plateau version of an oasis. Fifty-foot-high red stone cliffs sheltered narrow and elongated fields of corn, beans, melons, and fruit trees fed by a thin spring that ran the length of the canyon. The cliffs permitted nourishing sunlight to reach the fields, but held the drying wind at bay.

The expression on my face must have seemed to be one of wonderment. Eric looked my way and questioningly said, "Uh," as if to actually mean, "Didn't I tell you?" Everywhere else on the Plateau, the crops seem to fight back in a futile attempt to ward off their inevitable parched, desiccated demise. They struggle against lack of water, drying winds, intense summer heat, and rodents. The struggle has intensified during the last several years of an ongoing drought. Eric tells stories of Hopi farmers hand carrying water to their fields in 5-gallon buckets in an attempt to keep their precious corn plants alive. One farmer apparently had a brainstorm and ended up buying and installing a several hundred gallon metal cistern in the middle of his field. The cistern sat high above the ground on a tower. The tower quickly became the butt of jokes as well as ridicule focused on the how the farmer was apparently turning his back on the "Hopi Way" of praying for the katchina to bring rain. One day, however, the farmer came out to his field located below one of the mesas only to find that one of the many dust devils that dance across the Plateau had knocked over his tower. The cistern can still be seen nearly 200 yards away from where it originally fell over. It rests as a rusting reminder of testing the spirit world.

In the canyon that Eric and I had made our way to, both Navajo and Hopi farmers were raising crops that showed little sign of resistance to the elements. Rivulets and small hand-dug channels delivered spring water to the roots of the flourishing plants. The only battles they seemed to be fighting were against each other's leaves trying to bask in as much sunlight as possible. On that day, the scene in this canyon was unusual. Between Peabody Coal's sucking from the aquifer underneath the ground and the ongoing drought, many springs that once fed similar agricultural oases around the Plateau were dry. There is little chance that the fields that once fed Hopi and Navajo families near these springs will ever return. The spring where Eric and I stood seemed to be persevering. Nearby at the community of Moenkopi, the Moenkopi Wash also served to keep larger scale Hopi fields fed. As Eric and I stood there sweating in the heat, I couldn't help wondering whether in these small fields were stored memories that one day would be needed in order to ensure the future of humanity's ability to feed itself.

Global climatic destabilization is already testing how we raise and distribute our food. During the final weekend of 2006, a storm dropped over 2 feet of fresh snow on the unprepared region that connects Santa Fe and Albuquerque, New Mexico. At first, local residents welcomed the somewhat unusual weather. The region had experienced below normal precipitation for several years, and any moisture was welcomed. In little time however, it was realized that delivery trucks could not make the 45-mile trek from Albuquerque up to Santa Fe. The single interstate was iced over, and the state and county road crews were little match for the heavy and deep snow. By the fourth day of this weather event, the shelves at the grocery stores in Santa Fe were looking bare. The local newspaper reported on the growing crisis and focused on how people were most curiously concerned with the fact that they could not find eggs in the stores. The storm that challenged Santa Fe's ability to get eggs exemplified the fragility of today's food strings. It takes very little unusual weather to snap them. At the moment, current agribusiness is not prepared for whether and when climate shifts catastrophically challenge food chains and growing conditions. The small fields on the Colorado Plateau represent the human ability to raise food in the strictest of conditions. Sometimes on the Colorado Plateau, cultural memory, youthful exuberance, and innovation can create conditions suitable for growing food. Part of our resilient food future may be housed in a small nonprofit in Arizona.

The nonprofit Native Movement is headquartered in Flagstaff, Arizona. Its youthful director, Evon Peter, is an elder among a staff and group of consultants and volunteers with a median age of about 23. They are Hopi, Navajo, Jewish, mixed blood, and Alaskan Native. In resilience theory, they represent the small memory loop that feeds back into the larger loop where innovation, based on long-term knowledge and understanding, generates new knowledge and practices gleaned from traditions that worked, but also no longer work or are failing to stand up to current conditions. Like other sensitive youth from their generation, Evon and crew were tired of passively watching their home communities continue to deteriorate from increasing rates of nutrition-related diseases, devastating land management policy, and an education system irrelevant to the needs of Native youth. With shoestring budgets, volunteers, and lots of in-kind donations, they have been bringing together Native youth and elders. The latter have been working in concert to reinvigorate agricultural programs and affordable and alternative housing projects connected to local school programs on and off their home reservations on the Colorado Plateau and in locations away from the reservations, but where Native people still reside.

The mountain bike looked a bit tall for me at first. Its elaborate paint job was buried under layers of caked mud resulting from the owner's forays into the woods. We managed to lower the seat to align with the shortness of my legs. My host, Native Movement, had decided that this was the most appropriate manner in which to view its community agricultural projects located in several empty lots throughout Flagstaff. Fortunately, I am an avid bicycle rider. Riding around Flagstaff at near 8,000 feet after having been living in the Bay Area was not too much of a challenge.

My riding companion and guide was John Ramey. His twenty something lungs had little trouble with the altitude. His quicker reflexes seemed well suited for the requirements of urban mountain bike riding. John was a former student of mine. I did not remember him at first. He was one of those quiet students that often become filler in larger college classrooms: the kind that comes to class most of the time, do all their assignments, perform adequately on exams and quizzes, but never ask questions or bring attention to themselves. Teachers often are unaware of the impact we may have on some students as we ramble on and theorize about what should happen and needs to happen in the real world. In John's case, he obviously paid attention and applied to his life many of the things I had discussed in class. He had moved from Durango, Colorado, where he was a student at Fort Lewis College, to Flagstaff and began working with Evon and Native Movement. John was the community agriculture coordinator for what the organization called the Edible Landscape project.

Somehow, I managed to keep up with John and followed him to an Edible Landscape plot nestled among Ponderosa trees north of downtown Flagstaff. The plot sat next to an adult education facility. Many of the students at the facility were interested in the project and had participated in some of its construction. The plot was about the size of a small soccer field: the kind that local soccer leagues arrange for younger children, who have shorter legs, just learning the game. It was early spring, so nothing was growing yet in the plot except some early herbs that were springing up through the straw strewed about the plot in order to preserve as much moisture as possible in the soil. We donned the bicycles again and made our way across town to another plot. This one was half the size of the first, yet held more biomass and diversity. A local wealthy landowner had donated the smaller plot. It was situated in an older neighborhood of Flagstaff. Fruit trees guarded corners of the fenced-in plot and shaded many of the useful herbs and other foods already embraced by the old fence and walls of the nearby homes. It reminded me of the small gardens that one sees in older Hispano neighborhoods of Tucson, south of Phoenix, Albuquerque, and in parts of Chihuahua City. These small gardens not only reflect someone's herbal and fresh greens sanctuary but also act as a location of diversity. One can spy endemic plants in these places and often discover migratory birds and unique pollinators occupying their small niches.

The property that my grandparents owned and in which I was partially raised in southern California was one such refuge. The land grew figs, apricots, peaches, plums, prickly pear, corn, chilis, greens, squashes, and various herbs and flowers that my grandmother carefully nurtured. Much of the food ended up on our dinner plates or was given to family and neighbors. Songbirds and other birds visited the property, as did different kinds of small rodents and mammals. Today, an apartment complex covers the land. Those fruit trees will never again bring smiles and sticky fingers to young mischievous boys. When I recall those times, I am transported to my childhood when my cousins and I occupied much of our time exploring and becoming intimate with the geography of our landscape. These were precious and important times during our development. Gary Nabhan reminds us, in *The Geography of Childhood*, that "intimate places mean more to . . . children, and to others, than all the glorious panoramas I could ever show them." This is because there is "sense of comfort" that arrives with tiny shelters and with enclosed, but familiar places. There is an animal instinct to nest, to lie snug, and to be hidden. These places, Gary reminds us, are "endowed with a sense of refuge." Perhaps this was why the second plot in Flagstaff, the one surrounded by a fence and protected by the elder-like fruit trees, was more appealing. It had become a place of refuge.

The name *Native Movement* is ironically appropriate, considering the purpose of the local plots. Native people have also sought economic refuge in communities away from their home reservations. Today's employment discontinuities forces Native peoples into a mobile existence, shifting their living conditions to where there is appropriate work, better education for their children, and housing. In the case of many Hopi, Navajo, Pai, and Apache, this means moving to places such as Flagstaff, Winslow, Phoenix, Tucson, and Albuquerque. They are away from home, but still close enough to return on the weekends for ceremony or just to help out at sheep camp. Native people often choose to live in neighborhoods already occupied by other Native populations with whom they can share commonalities. Often these families arrive in their new situation with the intention to reach a certain economic plateau and then return back to the "rez." However, circumstances often do not permit the return trip. As a result, there is a diaspora of sorts that has created off-reservation communities in larger Southwestern towns as well as in the Mexican cities of Chihuahua City, Hermosillo, Ciudad Juárez, Cuahutémoc, and Tijuana. As the Native communities have become increasingly entrenched, second- and third-generation offspring are being raised in urban situations. These "urban Indians" learn little of their language and even less of what life is like on the landscapes they hear about in their elders' stories. But according to Calvin Long, a Hopi activist and consultant with Native Movement, it doesn't take much to remind young Native people what it means to be Native and to instill pride in their heritage, even when they are away from their historical homelands.

Calvin and I climbed up the winding trail leading to one of the lower peaks of the San Francisco Peaks just outside Flagstaff. His wide frame blocked the narrow trail as he walked ahead of me. He had to stop and turn to his side to let pass the occasional descending trail runner or hiker. We reached a wide and long meadow, took

a water break, and then crossed the meadow to a stand of Ponderosa pines and aspen. Sheltered by the trees were several large basal-
tic boulders. These rocks were most likely a result of recent volcanic
activity that had helped shape today's San Francisco Peaks. According to Hopi oral history, the volcanic activity on the Peaks was the
result of a young kachina that had fallen in love with a young, beau-
tiful, but mortal Hopi girl. When he realized that he could never
marry her, he became angry and had a kachina temper tantrum,
causing the volcanic activity.

I had first met Calvin Long in an Indian restaurant in San Rafael,
California. He is hopeful that he and Native Movement can network and encourage the next generation of stewards on the Colorado Plateau. The rocks amid this stand represented something else
to Calvin. He said that he comes here and sits among the rocks
when he needs to regather his thoughts. The stand is his refuge. He
also brings Native youth groups to this place to help them begin
the process of regaining and reactivating their connection to their
heritage and landscape. Calvin explained to me that even if young
Native people can no longer live in their home communities, they
can still gain a sense of place through short wilderness ventures and
through seeking and creating places of refuge. Offering local sustainable food for Native peoples living away from their home communities can act as refugia. The Native Movement plots are an experiment for similar local community projects that could dot
neighborhoods throughout the Southwest.

The young activists aligned with Native Movement are not the
only people devising ways to create agricultural refugia. In many
ways, this is not an innovation. Southwestern farmers have nearly
always maintained what might be considered backup or built-in
safety systems for when the rains failed to arrive or for whatever
reasons their crops did not produce in any given season. Tarahumara farmers today still plant fields high above the canyon rim, but
like the ancestors have done for centuries, they still plant small milpas along the angled walls of the canyon. Ak-Chin farmers in the
Sonoran Desert hedge their bets by planting along washes that will
likely flood during summer monsoon rains; Pueblo farmers still
plant larger fields near the village while, at the same time, planting

smaller fields near arroyos and in other places where water naturally sinks or flows after summer rains. Some Hopi communities would plant early in the season and sometimes later in the season in order to allow for early frosts, late frosts, or perhaps early or later rains. In some cases, they would locate ideal places for their crops at a distance in order to allow for minute regional variations in precipitation and other factors. Down south near Sedona, Arizona, this practice remains a sign of resilient thinking.

Sedona has gained a reputation for being a New Age haven for wealthy alternative healers, its energy vortexes, and the plethora of shops selling turquoise and silver jewelry. Remove the reputation, however, and the landscape is one of red-tinged stark beauty. The breathtaking canyons are formed by a couple of creeks that flow from the Colorado Plateau on their course toward dry oblivion or toward the Verde Valley farther south and west. As I drove west from Highway 17, the high red cliffs that rose above Sedona in the distance dominated my view. Closer, on the other side of my raised windows, passed juniper/piñon woodland understoried by red soil, cholla, and sagebrush. My windows were raised against the heat already accumulating by midday. I couldn't help but think of the group of nonnative men that had formed a dance group back in 1921. Members of the group were from Prescott and Sedona. They weren't doing the Texas two-step or an early form of line dancing. They had donned Hopi-looking regalia and had learned how to dance Hopi dances, including the very esoteric and sacred snake dance. They performed each year at the rodeo grounds in Prescott with the intention of preserving an art form they considered in decline and in danger of disappearing forever. These men called themselves the Smoki. In 1935, they even opened a museum as a way to help preserve Native history and customs on the Colorado Plateau. Their dances continued for 70 years. Most Hopi had no idea what these men were doing or ignored them until 1990 when 100 Hopi picketed downtown Prescott and the rodeo grounds, which lead to the end of the Smoki dances. My thoughts had wandered in this direction because not all nonnative people that come in contact with Native culture look first to exploit or appropriate it. The person I was on my way to meet, Greg Glasco, represented one of a large group of people that have found a niche from where they work tirelessly to help Native institutions.

I was early, so I made a slight detour to a local coffee shop in Sedona. The walkways around the coffee shop were already buzzing with out-of-town tourists from whom locals keep their distance for fear of being trampled as the out-of-towners look everywhere but where they are walking. Inside the coffee shop, a young woman with tattoos and pierced eyebrows and tongue took my order. Along one wall was one of those racks that display thirty-odd tri-folded colorful pamphlets one sees in tourist areas. Each pamphlet advertised a different wonderful, enchanting, or exciting activity for families. I noticed a couple of pamphlets advertising jeep tours to the local vortex. I wondered to myself whether the tour included a spiritual ascension at an extra cost.

I managed to follow Greg's directions to our meeting place off the main highway entering into Sedona. I directed my rental car down through a narrow path shaded by cottonwood trees and willows. The area to where I was going was obviously near water, with much greenery and trees that stood in front of me in stark contrast to the reddish sandstone that characterizes so much of Sedona. In the heat of the day, this area felt about 10 degrees cooler due to the trees. I found myself in a narrow valley watered by Sedona Creek. On one side were some older, relatively nondescript houses, and on the other side was more housing separated by a few acres of farmland. I found Greg bent over under his large straw hat. His toothy grin greeted me from a distance. I stepped from my rental car and immediately felt at home among growing cornstalks, chilis, squashes, and other local foods. I was also enjoying the dry heat of the Sedona summer as it brushed up against the humidity of the irrigated field of heirloom foods. It turned out that this land where Greg and I were standing was owned by the television actor Ted Danson. It was irrigated by an old acequia that tapped the creek about a quarter mile upstream from where we stood and led the water along a narrow ditch to the edge of the fields. A neighbor that lived upstream of the fields took advantage of the water, as was evidenced by the fruit trees, lush shrubs, and crops he grew on the other side of a chain-link fence.

Greg enthusiastically explained to me how he had worked out a deal with the owner of the land and a handful of Hopi families to create a backup crop system for the Hopi families. The family members endure the up to 2-hour drive from the mesas in order to work the fields. Greg explained how they bring their entire families to work and play among the irrigated crops. The picture he painted as he described the kids playing among the corn reminded me of my youth when my cousins and I would climb my grandfather's fruit trees and sometimes bend over to sniff the spicy scent of the carnations that my grandmother grew next to her chiltepins. Our childhood geography was constructed partly by heirloom foods, flowers, and juicy figs picked fresh from the rubbery branches. Near Sedona was again evidence of how small fields can lead to large impacts on the Colorado Plateau and to the revitalization of resilient systems. The future of humanity's foodways will be ensured partly by people such as Greg and his Hopi partners, plus Kyril, Justin, and Hank, tirelessly plowing their neighbor's fields and helping Navajo youth become a part of the process. The future connects to the past through elders such as Eric, who keep the past alive through his stories and the stories recalled in every kernel of his blue corn, and by Native Movement activists, who are connecting the past to the future with each neighborhood plot that brings diversity to the doorsteps of displaced Native peoples.

The story of the Colorado Plateau cannot end without first introducing the reigning matriarch of local "gardening," Phyllis Hogan. Phyllis's key role today, among many, is that she manages traditional "gardens" located around the San Francisco Peaks and on the Plateau. Before *ethnobotany* became a recognized term in the popular media and population, Phyllis was practicing it. Before the notion of biocultural diversity became interesting and significant among ethnobiologists, anthropologists, and conservation biologists, Phyllis had already espoused its importance. And while educators and nongovernmental organizations (NGOs) were still trying to figure out how to include Native youth in local ethnobiological projects and educational programs, Phyllis was already training the next generation of traditional "gardeners."

Around the flanks of the San Francisco Peaks, near the Little

Colorado River, and in other various locations around the Colorado Plateau, there are places that Phyllis refers to as "garden." People have come to these places for centuries to collect medicinal and other useful plants. Some of the places are guarded by individuals, whereas other gardens are stewarded by extended families and even clan groups. Many plants are endemic to these gardens, being found only at that location. In the process of collecting the plants, people have "cultivated" the gardens through intentional pruning, coppicing, planting, and even small-scale burning. These human-induced impacts serve to attract more understory plants, small and large mammals, and certain local and migratory birds. In other words, the gardeners have enhanced the diversity of the landscape. During her many years of building trust with local Native knowledge holders, Phyllis has become privy to many of the locations where plants are collected. She guards her knowledge jealously, further adding to the trust of the Native people that she has earned.

Years ago, Phyllis saw that fewer young people were attaining herbal and plant knowledge or even knew that the small collection gardens existed. At the request of Native elders, she began training the next generation of plant specialists. Phyllis works now at the resilient juncture of slow and short-term memory.

Finally, I want to take you and travel now to another diverse place; a place where a biocultural revival is on the surface. This place is along the Salt Song Trail that stretches from southern Nevada into southeastern California. In the middle of a recent spring, I sat at the base of a huge natural stone alcove formed from the Old Woman Mountains in the Mojave Desert and watched Southern Paiute Salt Song singers beginning the process of singing a landscape back into life. Their singing was acting also to revitalize an entire lifeway: a way of being with a landscape and the identities of countless Paiute to come who also will sing to these mountains. Three young Coahuila Bird Song singers showed up to the gathering. They were not invited, but found out about the gathering and somehow found their way across the sandpit-like dirt roads to get to the location and asked permission to sing. They sang, sang, and were still singing three hours later. These songs being heard again after decades of being silent had emerged from a people that no one even knew existed anymore 30 years ago. Food, farming, refugia, resilience, and biocultural diversity cannot exist without the language, without community, and without those that speak it through their heartfelt words that uphold the cultures that give voice to the lands. The future of the Colorado Plateau begins in our hearts.

7

Highways of Diversity and Querencia in Northern New Mexico

THE MOSAIC OF green that carpets the Mad River Valley in west central Vermont peeked through the shifting layers of clouds and fog drifting below. I was slowly walking downhill toward the large red barn that is the combination meeting place, dining area, and working space for Knoll Farm, a 450-acre working farm run by Peter Forbes and his wife, Helen Whybrow. Knoll Farm is also the headquarters for the Center for Whole Communities. Peter, Helen, and a dedicated staff manage the farm and center for the purpose of hosting environmental and social justice leaders at weeklong retreats at which the participants meditate and engage in whole thinking dialogue. People are nominated by past alum and travel from across the country to stay in small tents, cabin tents, and yurts situated among the mixed Eastern deciduous forest on a steep shelf that crosses along the upper part of the property. Everyone has to head downhill toward the barn for breakfast and meetings. I was there to act as "yeast," to ensure through questions and other inputs that the dialogue remained alive and flowing. I had done this the previous summer. As a result, I had been asked to nominate participants for this summer. I had nominated both Miguel Santistevan and Paula Garcia. At the time, Miguel was the program coordinator for the New Mexico Acequia Association directed by

Figure 7.1 An acequia near Embudo, New Mexico.

Paula Garcia. Paula could not make the retreat, but Miguel happily and excitedly made his way to Vermont's Mad River Valley.

It was the first full day of the retreat. As I headed toward the barn, taking in the green and fluffy white show below me, I saw Miguel emerge from his tent downhill and about 60 yards ahead of me. He crawled out of the low entrance and was in the process of standing up. He never reached his full height. During the middle of rising, he looked below at the valley floor peeking through the clouds. I looked on as he stopped in a crouch, his arms open to his sides. His back was to me, but it was obvious by his gestures that he couldn't believe what the river valley and clouds were revealing to him. He crouched even lower and then turned his entire body to his left, then to his right, stopping each time to face the valley below as if to make sure that the scene was still there. He repeated this impromptu dance several times and then stopped when he noticed me walking toward him from above. Mornings at Knoll Farm are taken in silence until 10 a.m. Therefore, Miguel could only smile at me as I walked by. I smirked, gave him a knowing glance, and continued downhill through the tall grass toward the barn.

Later, I asked Miguel what his dance was all about. Several other retreat members were hanging around, already eager to hear another one of Miguel's fantastical stories. Never one to miss an opportunity to be the center of attention and to mix storytelling with lessons, Miguel explained in his low gurgling voice tinged with a New Mexican Chicano accent, "I am a dry land farmer. I raise corn and beans in a desert. I pray for any rain and dig ditches so that the water from the river can travel to my field. To wake up and see so much green and moisture is like a miracle just took place in front of me. I had to acknowledge that and dance." Miguel's description of how he and others like him farm the arid region of northern New Mexico was reflective of how Hispanos and Native peoples before them coaxed food from the landscape.

During the opening decade of the nineteenth-century, Spanish settlement in the northern extent of New Spain was developing. By 1821, Taos had become a provincial capital as well as a port for the burgeoning fur trade. All this activity was made possible by military movements against the Comanche years earlier and the Ute's willingness to maintain a form of mutual cooperation. Within two decades, the northern extent of New Spain's settlement was pushed farther north into what is today northern New Mexico and southern Colorado. This would be the northernmost limit of New Spain in what is today the American Southwest.

Spanish frontier life encouraged a unique dependence on the local plants and the development of an agricultural system that could adapt to the short and often dry growing season. Plants and crops were important to Spanish and later Mexican settlers. This is evidenced in the names of some of the villages: *Capulin* (chokecherry), *La Jara* (willow), *Alamosa* (cottonwood), and *Cebolla* (onion). The landscape was familiar to the settlers. They had experienced the dry arid region south into what is now Durango, Mexico. Plants such as *Alamosa* and *Capulin* reach their northern limits in the region of northern New Mexico. Yet some plants such as piñon, currants, blue grama grass, and big sagebrush were unfamiliar, because those were adapted to northern climes and high altitude. Fortunately, Pueblo cooperation introduced some plants and the system of dry land agriculture to the settlers, and a relationship with the landscape blossomed.

In turn, the newcomers brought with them an irrigation system that would transform the way people farmed and connected with the land. The Spanish introduced the acequia irrigation system. Acequias are really just small irrigation ditches that tap local streams and creeks of their life-giving waters. The ditches divert the water along a path that parallels the small fields managed by the numerous farmers. In the acequia system, the farmers that rely on the acequia waters are called *parciantes*. Mark Twain once said that "in the West, whisky is for drinking and water is for fighting over." During "good" years, which are less often these days, the *parciantes* happily share the acequia waters. They wait patiently for their turn to open the small gates that divert the water into their parcels. Water allocation is managed by the Mayordomo, who is elected by the community to portion out the allocations and to decide who should be allowed water and who might have to wait during the course of a dry season. During these times, the Mayordomo becomes both a local psychologist and a police officer. He has to be prepared to anticipate *parciantes* that feel that they are owed more of their allocated shared and therefore keep their gates open longer than they should. And at the same time, the Mayordomo must be able to mindfully explain to his neighbor why he can't have as much water as the person downstream. Somehow, the system has worked in northern New Mexico for nearly 400 years, feeding the small fields growing heirloom crops and acting as an adhesive of both community and landscape.

Community acequias connected the *vegas* (commons) with the small fields. The acequias not only became extensions of the rivers and small streams that flowed from the nearby mountains but also created outliers of new riparian zones that nurtured aquatic as well as plant life. The acequias became highways for plant migration and diversity, and provided a source of useful plants for the settlers. The ditches bring water, irrigate the land, and create habitat as well as community. They are refugia and avenues of resilient culture and practice.

Large-scale agriculture tends toward monocropping: growing primarily one crop and only one variety of that crop. It is efficient in the short term because all the irrigation tools and planting, weeding, and harvesting machinery are tooled for the single crop's idiosyncrasies; and the farmer is able to use a single herbicide to protect the crop. Monocropping can normally take place only on a very large scale of 60 acres; its side effect is that the fields tend to be devoid of any life except that of the single crop. Just pull off the highway that runs adjacent to large agribusiness fields in Iowa, Indiana, Colorado, and south of Phoenix. I have done this several times. Once in eastern Indiana, I was on my way to finding a fishing spot. I had given a talk about ethnobotany at Erlham College and had borrowed a car and a map from a student. I fished to little avail and decided to do some "antiquing." There were several of those large antique malls in the area advertised on huge billboards along Interstate 70. On the way to one, I had the impulse to stop and take in the over abundance of maize. Maize (corn) was everywhere, interrupted only by old farmhouses with faded paint and large harvesters. I stepped out of my car into the oppressive heat that felt like a steamy weight on my shoulders. The horizon ran green for miles and resembled corduroys. The air was silent except for the rustle of large leaves of corn as they brushed against each other in the light wind. Except for small willows, dock, and a handful of grasses that struggled in the ditches that separated the road from the field, there was nothing else growing. There weren't even any crows around to scold me at my invasion of their space. I have had many opportunities to walk and work in small-scale Native and Hispano cornfields where one feels invited to stroll among the wide, uneven rows. Around the monocropped fields, I felt no such invitation, except to jump back into my borrowed car and crank up the air-conditioning.

Back in New Mexico, the acequias were not the only source of new plants. The Europeans brought with them, sometimes purposefully and sometimes accidentally, Old World plants capable of surviving in the area. These plants were a source of familiarity and comfort to the settlers who found themselves in an unfamiliar environment. In addition, the indigenous people of New Spain accepted many of the new plants. Apple orchards sprung up on the narrow valley floors. Peaches became a favorite among the residents as well as apricots and Old World cherries. The settlers introduced melons to the Pueblo people as well as wheat and oats. Although many new crops came to the region with the settlers, they did not replace the abundance of food plants that had been grown in Rio Arriba for centuries before the first Old World peaches. Many of the heirloom as well as introduced crops are still being raised and enjoyed by people in northern New Mexico. Several variations of apples (*Malus*) are still grown in hidden orchards near Embudo, New Mexico. *Embudo* is a Spanish word for funnel, referring to the manner in which Embudo Creek springs from a narrow canyon that connects to the larger Rio Grande River. The elder statesman of New Mexican varieties of *Malus* is Juan Estevan Arellano. For the better part of the last 50 years, Juan has made it his mission to catalog and maintain the integrity of northern New Mexico's heirloom crops and the culture that relies on them. With the help of specialists from New Mexico State University's Sustainable Agriculture Science Center at Alcalde, New Mexico, Juan is able to search for heirloom orchards along what was the Spanish Camino Real (The Royal Road) that ran from Santa Fe, New Mexico, south into central Mexico during Spanish colonial times. Juan and the researchers believe the Spanish may have brought up to 100 fruit varieties to this region of the world; these include not only apples but also apricots, pears, cherries, plums, and peaches. According to Juan's studies of ancient records and texts, the Spanish scattered fruits all along the Camino Real. Some are found standing in people's backyards and at the edge of *suertes*, the acequia-fed fields. In most cases, the landowners have no idea that that an old tree producing those sweet yellow apples are ancient and heirloom. Apples that are included in Juan's growing and extensive catalogs are a reddish, tart Baldwin apple growing near Hondo, New Mexico; a Grimes golden apple surviving on a single tree in Santa Fe; and a tree on the Salinas Pueblo Missions National Monument that produces a yellow apple and is more than 100 years old. As with other heirlooms, a nostalgia accompanies them. However, preserving heirlooms is crucial for the integrity of our food future. So many of these heirloom apples, for example, are disease resistant, insect resistant, drought resistant, and also produce qualities perfect for storage, baking, and just plain old eating.

Juan has grafted some of these varieties onto the fruit trees that occupy precious space in his 2.4-acre garden along the Rio Embudo. Juan's garden is not your average garden. He seems to have been able to plant, sow, transplant, and graft food varieties from nearly every continent with which his Indo-Hispanic ancestors came in contact. And like the gardens of people in northern New Mexico, who had never been trained by the U.S. Department of Agriculture (USDA) Extension Office or Burpee Seed Company to plant in parallel rows and to erase any sign of weeds, his patches of native raspberries, apples, chilis, edible greens, and squashes are arranged in no particular order. The fruit trees, including his apples, are planted in the *alito*, the space below the acequia. This is said to be the best place to grow fruit trees due to the waters that seep through the unlined acequia.

Fruit trees are not the only heirloom crops that remain in abundance in northern New Mexico. The iconic chili is grown in people's dooryard gardens in places such as Arroyo Seco as well as in large industrial-size productions such as the ones found in and around Hatch, New Mexico. It seems, however, that when non–New Mexican and non–chili heads consider New Mexico chili, they refer to either the Big Jim Green or the Chimayo Red. The Big Jim chili is a familiar variety with its long fruit, tangy mild flavor, and most important, its relatively large inner cavity that is ideal for stuffing with cheese and other ingredients that go into making chili rellenos. The Chimayo chili remains an important care package insert that my friends from New Mexico mail to me at my California home. But New Mexico also harbors several other varieties of chili, such as the mild Alcalde green chili, the sweet Cochiti and Velarde green chilis, and the Escondida red and Jemez red chilis. These varieties represent only a few that are available and grown in New Mexico. I suspect that, like Juan's apples, there are as many chili varieties hiding in people's backyards and at the edge of their bean fields as there are known varieties. The point here is that growers, families, and even large industrial managers select for spiciness, flavor, and shape when they grow their food crops, further extending the library of our food choices. And with each selection rises the opportunity for genetic shift and overall species resistance to those nasty things that nature might throw at them. The same can be said for corn, beans, and squashes.

I will not venture into the historical and social complexities that caused the Spanish to be forcibly ejected by the Native inhabitants from northern New Spain in 1680, but 12 years later the Spanish returned. Relations between the invaders and Natives were still not perfect, but social and cultural interchange flourished, including the interchange of foods. Corn is a prime example of this interchange. For example, somewhere along the aromatic lineage of New Mexico's food heritage, people acquired the taste for small, wrinkled, dried corn called chicos. Sometimes, the individual kernels are dark due to the occasional roasting they received before being dried. Later, the chicos are cooked in recipes with beans, different meats, vegetables, and of course with chili. The process and unique flavor are so unique to New Mexico that Slow Food USA's Ark of Taste project has included chicos. Any corn variety can be dried to become chicos, but some are better suited to the process, such as the Rio Lucio Concho corn.

New Mexico's corn varieties alone would make the region an ideal nominee for Slow Food's Ark of Taste. Still being grown and eaten are the following: the Truchas Lumbroso, Nambe Pueblo, and Vadito white flint and posole corn; Rio Chama Red corn; Escondida and Taos blue; Isleta Pueblo White; and the Hernandez Red Mix corn. And the list does not end with corn varieties. Bean lovers appreciate golden-colored beans from the Four Corners area, Appaloosa pintos, and Colorado bolita beans. Lamb's-quarters, also known as quelites, are encouraged in people's fields and gardens; others still grow heirloom varieties of Peñasco cheese squash and Rio Lucio pumpkins, whereas north of Taos a variety of red wheat still goes into the ground each year, but only by two farmers up near the small community of Questa. Once, when I was visiting the area with Ernie Atencio, he planned to take me over to meet with Patty Martinson and Terry Badhand, the two gregarious directors of the Taos County Economic Development Corporation (TCEDC). This name evokes images of people in suits sitting at desks, figuring out ways to increase bank loans to underprivileged rural families. Well, that's what first entered my imagination when I heard the name of this outfit.

TCEDC occupies the offices of a medium-sized, nondescript building in a smallish industrial park south of Taos. I was there to consider funding some of its food-related projects. Despite its bureaucratic sounding name, TCEDC focuses on bringing opportunities for small-scale food producers in northern New Mexico to process and market their foods. The TCEDC, whose building houses a USDA-approved kitchen, recently put on the road New Mexico's first mobile *mostanza*: a butcher shop on wheels for the few remaining ranchers that still raise livestock, but cannot get them to the nearest slaughterhouse nearly 400 miles away. All its efforts are to keep the families that still sustainably manage the landscapes in northern New Mexico on their lands. Many of them are acequia farmers.

When Ernie and I entered the room where the meeting was taking place, I noticed a display of the foods that TCEDC's partners produce and market. Terry and Patty even made available many of them in the munchies and meal they provided for those in attendance. In the display, I noticed what looked like a 5-pound paper bag of wheat flour. They said the bag held flour grown by only two farmers north of Taos. It was a Taos Red wheat brought to the region by Spanish colonists and continually grown to this day. I suggested that I would love to take home a bag of the flour to include in my recipes. They were excited and said that they would make sure that I had a bag to take by the end of the meeting. We held our meeting, ate, and toured the large kitchen and then the offices. Ernie and I were ready to leave, and I went back to the meeting room where I had left my notebook and noticed a 50-pound bag of flour leaning against the chair where I had been sitting. When I acted surprised, Terry and Patty gleefully motioned that this was my gift of the flour. I think I said something like "Oh, my god, what I am going to do with this much flour?" I then expressed the good fortune that I had rented an SUV to drive back to California rather than fly back like I normally did for these trips. As it turned out, I had to negotiate a blizzard complete with frozen roads on my way home. The 50 pounds of flour in the back seat added some additional weight and stability to the car.

All of the crops just mentioned remain in production in New Mexico, but at a much smaller level than 200 to 300 years ago. As modernization has crept up on the Rio Arriba, so much agricultural knowledge has slipped away. A zesty example of modern threats to New Mexican agriculture is the one that threatens the New Mexico chili crop. Before the North American Free Trade Agreement (NAFTA) discarded tariffs between the United States, Canada, and

Mexico, and before the entrance of China and India into the World Trade Organization (WTO), which opened the doors of US agricultural markets to additional offshore producers in other parts of the world, New Mexico had solidly held the market for most chili pepper products. Except for spices such as paprika, varieties of Asian peppers, and mild pepper such as pimento, the world viewed New Mexico as the center of hot pepper production. It's not an accident that The Chile Pepper Institute is housed on the campus of New Mexico State University in Las Cruces. All over the state, chili pepper is harvested in small quarter-acre acequia-fed fields such as Miguel's and on large-scale agribusiness sites as seen at Rio Valley Chili, which harvests 12 million pounds of red chili each year. Today, however, 80 percent of the chili pepper products consumed by chili heads in the United States are imported. The central reason for this conundrum is cheap labor. Chili, and red chili especially, is best harvested by hand. Mechanized harvesters damage the delicate pods. Using mechanization then is only economically efficient on larger farms. Chili producers outside the United States can afford to pay their workers lower salaries for hand harvesting.

Although small traditional chili producers such as Miguel and Esteban will always plant and grow their unique heirloom varieties of chilis in northern New Mexico, larger scale chili producers will be forced to turn to genetically modified organism (GMO) chilis, which will be bred to withstand the impact of machine harvesting in order to compete with the labor forces of Zimbabwe, Peru, and India. At the moment, most GMO research has focused on the large and economically significant crops such as corn and cotton. Chilis apparently are not important enough for large-scale GMO research and for companies to pour money into the techniques to modify their genetic makeup, but that could soon change. According to the Texas Agricultural Experiment Station in Weslaco, Dr. Marla Binzell has developed a method to insert genes for the desired traits in chili peppers. This method could lead to better disease and insect resistance; better colors; increased stability; and, more important, lower heat levels; and processing features such as stems that readily separate from the pods for easier mechanical harvesting. It is at this juncture where the small-scale producers in the region will begin to be concerned. It wouldn't be long before terminator genes (genes in food crops modified to cause the second generation of a plant to be sterile) are blended into the mix and begin to threaten the heirloom varieties.

There were probably about 190 plants being used by Hispanos in this region up until about 1920. This number was arrived at after going over historic records, from herbal and ethnographic materials, and from speaking with elder herbalists and farmers. After 1920, it seems that plant knowledge began its slow decline. It was about this time when industry, cars, and electricity began to arrive in the region. In every formerly rural place throughout the world, the arrival of industry and access to modern medical practices open the door for the exit of traditional plant knowledge.

Along the Rio Arriba, most plant knowledge was stored in the minds of the plant specialists (herbalists, *curanderos*, and farmers), those respected and relied upon for their knowledge. But the knowledge was also available to the wives, grandmothers, and caring aunts of the region. Due to social changes, changes in eating habits, medical practices, and increasing modernization, less than half of the plant knowledge and uses of the past have survived. Although contemporary studies will highlight a great number of crops that Hispanos used to grow, the key to the estimate is whether or not the plants are still used. Many of these studies are based on secondary sources and are not derived from actual conversations with practitioners. Dependence on modern manufactured foods and medicines has virtually removed all knowledge of plants and agriculture in the layperson. In short, agricultural knowledge is obsolete.

Fortunately, the status of the *curandero* and of the farmer remains relatively lofty in Hispano culture. In most cases, plant knowledge is archived in families who have maintained the relationship to the land. Within the family, there often is a person who has chosen to hold on to the knowledge. Some Hispanos, mostly women, have chosen to relearn Hispano uses of plants. And in the case with Miguel, efforts are being made not to let this knowledge disappear. In fact, he hopes to revitalize acequia farming in northern New Mexico. Although the practice of and familiarity with farming are on the decline, along the Rio Arriba there remains recognition of a relationship to their place and of a legacy of stewardship.

Paula, Miguel, and several other people that comprise the New Mexico Acequia Association have been battling to keep the acequias flowing. For nearly a century, water rights have been stolen, appropriated, and legislated away from the small Hispano farmers in New Mexico. This is not a new story. Enchanting places such as northern New Mexico attract gentrification. New "ranchettes" near Santa Fe, Espanola, and Taos are reminders of the old chili fields and other agricultural operations that formerly fed Hispano families and sustained the diversity of the area. How then are people such as Juan, Ernie, Miguel, and Paula going to keep the *parciantes* on the lands and open those small acequia gates? Miguel's answer is focused on the youth.

Miguel's energy is magnetic. His eyes widen when he begins a story, causing one to stop everything so as not to miss any detail. It is no wonder that he has been able to attract Hispano youth to his efforts to build a new generation of acequia *parciantes*. For the last several years, Miguel's new *parciantes* have been raising heirloom crops such as red corn, chivita pinto beans, and chili. Using digital storytelling, they have been recording the remaining elder acequia farmers' shared experiences. From this, they have produced a monthly radio show broadcast into area homes. They have also convinced these kids to become engaged in advocacy for the acequias and in legislation on behalf of water rights. Miguel and Paula hope that these cadres of Hispano youth, whom they refer to as *semillas* (seeds), will inspire others to become engaged in their culture and land.

Human existence is imbued with plants, land, and water. A large part of the history of Hispanos in the Rio Arriba includes the same. Hispano social organization, spirituality, and aesthetics are permeated with the water that flows through the dry lands that nurtures their crops and consciousness. Since 1681, when the *Recopilación de leyes de los reynos de las indias* (The Laws of the Indies) were published and distributed throughout the New World, Hispano consciousness has been imbued with their landscape. The laws, in Book Four, Title Seven, Law Seven, ordered, "that land and surroundings, which are to be settled, be the most fertile, with abundant pasture, firewood, lumber, materials, sweet waters, natural people, transportation, ingress and egress, and there be no lake close by, nor marsh lands, where venomous animals live, nor there be any corruption of winds, or waters." According to Juan Estevan Arellano, this and two other laws lay the "cornerstones, the foundation of what has become," what he calls Hispano Querencia: that which affords his people a sense of place. Querencia is also simply the love for the land and place. But it is a much more complex concept that is based on a number of cognitive models unique to Hispano cognition along the Rio Arriba. The models include notions of language, cultural memory of place, and identity.

Along the Rio Arriba, there is an immediate emotional connection between a person's cognitive and physical landscape and his or her personal and ethnic identity. The interdependence that exists between Hispano culture and the land extends to plant history, which contributes to the survival of the culture stored in the collective memory.

Here we find that querencia emerges as a cultural adhesive, binding previously unconnected concepts. The inherent intercultural clash is recognized as one of the common sustaining elements among Hispanos that ties them to other Hispanos. The interdependence and cultural cohesion that today's Hispanos share is the recognition not only of a changing culture but also of an enduring landscape.

To Hispanos, querencia is a blend of mental spaces not only involving bioregionalism but also including emotional, spiritual, cultural, and ecological health. When people think of land, the concept is enmeshed with notions of cultural memory. These and other mental spaces merge into a multidimensional blended space, which is applied to understanding how the Hispano concept of cultural memory is directly tied to the landscape. The environment is not a thing for Hispanos but is a part of their identity because their memories—encoded in their languages, songs, ritual, stories, and cultural history—are linked to their place.

The stories, also called *cuentos*, explain and store Hispano memories of connections to the landscape. They afford life and meaning to the cultural history with the land as well as to a sense of belonging to a place. Without *cuentos*, there is no sense of where the people have been with a place and no sense of where they are going.

The commons are especially dear to Hispano land conceptualizations as well as to traditional land management. The commons are commonly used and managed lands surrounding Hispano villages and towns. Many are parts of centuries-old land grants and today are often located in national forests and sometimes on private lands. In the past, villagers collectively used these lands to graze livestock, hunt, and gather firewood and useful plants. Many feel that to lose some of the commons has been akin to having lost a part of their connection to the land. Hence, the memories of the lands cannot be transferred to their children. They feel then that to lose their place is to lose themselves. Joe Gallegos of San Luis, Colorado, mentions when referring to the nearby privately and publicly controlled mountain that was once a part of the commons of San Luis that "it will never really feel like we are home, not as long as the mountain is under lock and key."

Now, all of this mental–cognitive–linguistic stuff doesn't mean that all Hispanos in New Mexico go about uttering to themselves The Laws of the Indies and the notions of querencia. But if one were to listen closely to local conversations, the choice and use of words and symbols, and the meanings, the emotional connections would emerge. The words make available not only mental inferences but also emotions and novel patterns of action and practice.

Patterns of land use in northern New Mexico and southern Colorado have gone through extensive changes during the last 200 years of Spanish, Mexican, and then US occupation. The Europeans introduced cattle, sheep, and other livestock. They also brought with them new agricultural techniques. Both introductions permanently altered existing pre-Columbian land use and subsistence practices. American Indian and Hispano agriculturalists somehow adjusted to the changes through mixed ranching, farming, and limited use of the commons. However, fluctuations with regard to the amount of grazing, stocking, large- and small-scale ranching, and government-imposed restrictions and regulations have made it difficult to maintain a sustainable land use system.

What has really changed and had the largest impact on the landscape is Hispano access to the land and its precious water. The land and management of its resources have been transformed dramatically as a result of the numerous and tangled water laws, restrictions on both private and public lands, and protected private property. Large tracts of what were once lands held in common for locals to gather wild plants and to graze their livestock on are now privately and federally owned. The result is that Hispano families and communities have been displaced from the land. The last few generations of New Mexican Hispanos then have not had the opportunity to acquire a land ethic, such as querencia, on which to base their identity. Another significant element that must be addressed here is that Hispano displacement from the land and from being able to raise much of their own food comprises a form of environmental racism.

Populations of Hispanos in northern New Mexico, as well as populations of American Indians living on most reservations, live in food deserts: geographic regions with limited access to diverse and nutritious foods. Ease of acquisition of prepackaged foods outweighs access to ancestral and healthy foods. Another important element is that even those who remain close to lands that their ancestors managed have little time to work the land. Unless one owns a very large tract of arable land, a small-scale subsistence lifestyle is extremely difficult economically. Many Hispanos are forced to work several local jobs or commute one to two hours away to work in the larger New Mexico communities. When asked, most will say they just don't have time to go pick or grow plants when they can find a remedy or food in the medicine cabinet or the refrigerator. An unfortunate outcome for much of the younger generations is that land-based knowledge is unnecessary to them. It is "old fashioned" and not a part of the "street culture." But it is exactly the old-fashioned stuff—the long-term memory spoken of in resilience theory—that, coupled with short-term memory loops such as those being engendered by Juan and Miguel, is going to keep the heirloom Hispano culture vibrant and alive along the Rio Arriba. Unlike many American Indian groups today, wherein one would have difficulty finding a person who knows anything about plants, the knowledge survives to a degree among Hispanos in this region. Specialists can be found in nearly every village and hamlet, and even the layperson will have samples of Osha, *Manzanilla*, *yerba buena*, and perhaps Inmortal. A relationship remains; relationships much like the ones that Miguel Santistevan and Juan Estevan Arellano have maintained. As mentioned earlier, when one listens to them speak, one is really listening to their stories.

Story is at the core of community resilience. It comprises the matter, substance, and adhesive of human capital. Stories communicate our values through the language of our heart and our emotions. Stories are what we feel. They express our hopes, our cares, and our obligations. In northern New Mexico, enough of the viable land remains in which the story of querencia can be housed. It will require individuals such as Miguel, Juan, and Ernie Atencio, among many others, to re-story the land and its people. Biodiversity is linked to cultural diversity. The link will remain vibrant as long as the land-based stories, metaphors, cultural models, and other ways of talking about the land continue. They will work to ensure that the supporting framework of cultural diversity remains viable.

8

Singing to Turtles, Singing for Divine Fire

EFRAIN WAS SITTING alone in the shade of a medium-height cotton-wood tree. He and the tree shared the space at the edge of Victor Masayesva's farm on the Hopi reservation in northern Arizona. Except for the handful of cottonwood and peach trees, the rust-colored land here was washed in the midday sun. Efrain seemed very content to be in the shade on the warm Colorado Plateau day. The others had moved near Victor's house to look at baskets and some of the seeds being saved by the Masayesvas. Efrain was part of a small group of Seri Indians visiting the Hopi reservation as part of a cultural exchange. Heat and stark landscapes are nothing new to the Seri. The Seri homeland is located along the eastern shore of the Sea of Cortez on the Sonoran coast of Mexico. The title of one of my favorite books about the Seri, Where the Desert Meets the Sea (by David Yetman), describes succinctly the nature of their homeland. On the way to join the crowd near the house, I caught in the corner of my squinting view Efrain by himself and decided to offer a little company. On my way over, I wondered how he had ended up under the tree. He must have asked someone to help him find a chair and place it and him in the shade. Efrain is blind. As I got closer, I noticed that, despite his blindness, he was squinting in the midday sun. He adjusted his view toward my direction and smiled as I neared. I stood before him and greeted him in Spanish. He returned the greeting and widened his smile, showing a full set

Figure 8.1 Seri Elder in Desemboque, Sonora, Mexico.

of teeth that stood in contrast to his very dark skin. Efrain must have been in his late seventies, but still displayed signs of vigor despite his lack of sight. Efrain gestured in my direction and stated more than asked in Spanish, "You're an Indian, aren't you?" I said yes, and before I could say the name of my tribal affiliation, he said, "You're Tarahumara." Again, I said yes, and then he said in a very knowing and sage-like manner, "I have been waiting for you."

I followed the chill climbing from the base of my spine as it made its way up to my shoulders, across my neck, and ended at the crown of my head. The last time I had felt a similar chill was when the Hopi elder at Moenkopi told me that my students and I were fulfilling Hopi prophecy. It was a good thing that Efrain could not see because I am certain that my eyes widened upon the surprised expression on my face. Efrain explained that he had fasted for this trip. He knew somehow that, for him, the trip would be more than a cultural exchange. As a result of his fast, he learned also that he would encounter a Native person in the United States, but that the person would be indigenous to Mexico. It was to this person, he explained, that he would impart some songs. It turned out, however, that I had to learn the songs in Seri country.

I didn't agree immediately to learn new songs. I was still in shock that I was appearing in this elder's visions. He shifted the conversation to the stars. He asked what my people knew about the constellations and whether we had songs about them. I told him what little I knew, and he seemed very pleased that something was there. The others were motioning for us to join them near the house, but before I helped Efrain slowly walk over there, he made me promise that I would visit him in Seri country. I agreed. What else could I do?

Later that day, I told my friend, Laurie Monti, about the exchange I had had with Efrain. She and her husband, Gary Nabhan, were the US escorts for the Seri group. Both of them have been living among and learning ethnoecology, ethnoherpetology, and ethnobotany from the Seri since the 1970s. No American research team has been more intimate with the Seri, yet even Laurie and Gary always suggest that they still understand very little about these unique and amazing people. After telling Laurie about the visit, she smiled knowingly, chuckled, shook her head, and said something to the effect, "That's Efrain." Laurie suggested that I make the trip to Desemboque, located in the Mexican state of Sonora along the coast of the Sea of Cortez. Six months later, I was driving along a dirt road, heading north, in the middle of the incredible Sonoran Desert, thornscrub to my right and azure-blue waters to my left, wondering whether I had made a wrong turn.

The Seri have lived on and have managed their split of coastal land along the Mexican states of southern Sonora and northern Sinaloa for over 2000 years. They have also occupied a handful of islands off the coast, most notably Tiburon Island. The sophistication and complexity of Seri oral tradition and extensive place names on both the mainland and the islands are reflections of their long-standing relationship to their homeland. The small bands of Seri have survived first the Spanish entradas, then brief civil rebellions, and later Mexican colonialism. Today, they number about 600 tribal members, but have numbered as high as 2,000 in the past. By the mid-nineteenth century, the Mexican government had declared the Seri coast to be public land, and the Seri increasingly found themselves hemmed in by Mexican ranching and fishing operations. In 1965, they were evicted from Tiburon Island, which had been declared a wildlife preserve. In 1975, however, a 56-kilometer strip of mainland coast was designated a Seri *ejido*, lands held in common by the members of the *ejido*. The Seri were also given formal title to Tiburon Island, although their use of it is still restricted.

In the interceding time before this trip, I had received a surprise package in the mail. It came in a beat up-box with a return address from Flagstaff, Arizona. When I opened it, I knew immediately what a special gift I had received: a handwoven Seri basket about 6 inches tall and perhaps 10 inches across. It was of the classic Seri basket style whereby the sides of the basket are larger than the small opening. It looked as though someone had taken a taller round basket and sat on it, causing the sides to bulge out. Seri women are known for their basket-weaving skills. Many are woven so tightly that they hold water. In the past, people cooked stews and porridge-type foods in these baskets. What made this one unique was that it was primarily black.

Seri baskets are an ideal container in the desert for carrying things such as wood, herbs, plant foods, meat, and washing. Baskets were used for winnowing grains and for their storage later. They're like a plant-based suitcase or even a garbage can. The modern Seri, however, have become accustomed to contemporary containers made of plastic, glass, metal, and ceramics. As a result, basket making has declined and become a craft devoted more toward a cash economy for the few tourists that somehow find their way to the two main Seri villages. Seri baskets are very sturdy. The inner coil and central support system are made of split torote, which is a type of tree. The bundles are wrapped with the inner bark of torote stems. Due to the wrapping material, most Seri baskets are light tan in color, unless some of the stems' materials have been dyed a rust red with the root bark of the plant species of Krameria, called *cósahui* in Seri and commonly known as white ratany. This is why my black gift basket was unusual. Sometimes, the weavers use split devil's claw for decoration. Unlike Pima and O'odham baskets, which weave in split devil's claw seed pods for decoration, the Seri used dye plants to color their weaving materials. These include limberbush (*Jatropha cuneata*), mesquite (*Prosopis sp.*), red mangrove (*Rhizophora sp.*), and sometimes a recipe of several plants called *haat an ihahóopol*, translated from the Seri as "limberbush in what-one-blackenswith." The ingredients are sea blite (*Suaeda moquinii*), *xeescl*, desert lavender (*Hyptis emoryi*), *heejac* (*Pithecelobium* confine), and pomegranate rind (*Punica* sp.). The plain-colored wrapping material became the source for decorations. A handwritten note written by Laurie was lying at the bottom of the basket; it said Efrain's wife, Maria, had made the basket and that it was a gift for me. The note also stated that the decorations depicted the Seri night sky. More chills. Handmade baskets are more than tourist purchases or grist for decorating the edges of ethnographic-related museum exhibits. Baskets represent the stuff of resilience. In my hands, I now held resilience in a black Seri basket.

Today, basketry is more an art than an element of subsistence, more a reflection of a community's sustainable impact on its local ecosystem than stuff to decorate shelves with. The resilience was not stemming from the sustainable harvesting practices and subconscious thought that went into the collection of the materials. Nor was it a result of the Seri community's ability to adapt to changing economic forces so that their baskets have transformed from an object of subsistence to a commodity. Rather, the basket symbolized Efrain's recognition that his culture's ability to creatively survive all the known and unknown forces threatening the Seri way of life will depend partly on the endurance, process, and performance of Seri songs. Baskets create space for other more resilient parts of Seri culture to flourish.

Seri folks seem to be poised to sing at any given moment. They will even sing to moments. While waiting for dinner to come to our tables at the Hopi Cultural Center's restaurant on Second Mesa, our Seri guests suddenly broke into song. While driving at 100 miles per hour across a salt flat south of Desemboque, my Seri passengers broke into song in order to protect us. During my visits to Seri villages, singing often accompanies dancing in the evenings. To the Seri, singing and songs are multifaceted expressions of their multidimensional relationship to space, to situation, to emotion, to manifestation of the supernatural in a local place, and to the continuing renewal of all the above. To sing is to be alive, to be connected to and a part of what is alive, and in many ways this sums up Seri spirituality.

In *Singing the Turtles to Sea*, Gary Nabhan notes that Seri boatmen sing songs while traversing to an island as "Seri life insurance." The songs are sung to placate the serpent beneath the waters that might stir up large waves and unpredictable currents, which could sink or destroy the small boats that the Seri manage in the unsteady waters of the Sea of Cortez. In a way, Nabhan's joking remark is an accurate analogy of Seri songs and singing. Efrain was hoping that I would learn his star songs as a way to ensure their survival. Of course, I could not refuse.

My inability to refuse was what led me to my current situation driving along an unknown dirt road in a remote part of Sonora. Fortunately, I was not alone. My friend Celia Lowenstein had asked to accompany me on this trip. She is a filmmaker and wanted to visit Seri country in search of new film ideas, particularly musical ones. We met up in Tucson. I had a relatively new SUV owned by The Christensen Fund. It was comfortable in its over-the-top exuberance. We stocked up on road-tested munchies at a nearby health food chain in Tucson and headed south into the Sonoran Desert through the border point of Nogales. The plan was to meet Laurie Monti in the seaside community of Kino Bay after first stopping in Hermosillo to take care of some Christensen Fund-related meetings that I had lined up. Except for a brief fiasco at the checkpoint south of the border, the drive was uneventful. The Mexican authorities needed better proof that I had permission to drive the over-the-top SUV that was owned by a private family foundation south into Mexico. I ended up having to call someone back at the office to fax a hastily written and signed let-ter of permission to the authorities there at the checkpoint. The fax seemed to convince them that I was not actually driving this vehicle into Mexico in order to sell it on the black market, and we were on our way again.

The diversity of the Sonoran Desert seems more obvious the farther south one travels through its namesake Mexican state. It's as though the varieties of animal and plant life feel less constrained to express their voices and show off their ability to happily flourish underneath such a hot sky. As we head farther south, the geology underlying the cacti and amphibians became less Basin and Range and more canyon, riparian, and craggy. The diversity of the landscape influences the diversity of the plant and animal life. In the past, the biodiversity was accompanied by cultural diversity. The current state of Native America in the Greater Southwest reflects only a remnant of what used to be. In 1535, when Cabeza de Vaca and his lost companions stumbled their way along the Sierra Madre, following Native rumors that other white men had been seen farther south, they were watched and sometimes greeted by numerous economically rich peoples with equally rich tribal names: Jova, Concho, Opata, Endeve, Jumano, Suma, Chinipa, Acazee, Temoris, and Xixime. Linguists suggest that most were Uto-Aztecan speakers, whereas some such as the Jumano were most likely Athabascan. The people managed and flourished in their desert landscapes, which only slightly resemble today what they used to look like. Most were agriculturalists, taking advantage of the large and small rivers that flowed through the region. Cabeza de Vaca and later visitors such as Diego de Guzman and Fray Marcos de Niza all marveled in their journals at the variety and abundance of foods harvested from the desert by the people that they encountered, killed, and tried to convert. They mentioned numerous kinds of corn, beans, squashes, and fruits as well as the various ways that the foods were prepared. Going over these accounts, I can't help but wonder what cultural knowledge was lost when the string of epidemics cleared the land of the people that had helped it to thrive. Were their methods of growing foods in the desert, ones that we could still use today: innovative irrigation techniques, wonderful and tasty food pairings, varieties of pest-resistant domesticates forever lost, and understandings of agroecology that would help modern desert dwellers co-inhabit their place in a more resilient manner? It's easy to become depressed when thoughts such as these skirt the edges of one's attention at 80 miles per hour. Instead, I choose to consider how the knowledge held by the peoples that remain may lend a hand toward contemporary resilient communities. That can become depressing as well, but at least it's action that one can delve into today.

Many communities still occupy this landscape. They are likely descendants of some of the tribal nations listed previously. Is it possible that remnants of the food and food knowledge from the past remain stored in the language, family recipes, and some backyard gardens? The answer is in the pudding or, in this case, the salsa. Putting aside that Mexican-styled salsa surpassed ketchup a few years as the most likely condiment to be found on a kitchen table in the United States, most salsas sold in grocery stores do not resemble those found on the dining table of Mexicans. If we remain in Sonora, the spiciness of the US versions pales in comparison. No offense, but most US salsas are simply way too coarsely unusual for the refined palates of Mexican eaters. US salsa designers seem to feel that if they add more exotic ingredients to the recipes that their salsas are worth eating. However, they tend to be a bit too artsy in their approach. Ask a Mexican from Sonora to put pineapple, black beans, mango, or corn into a salsa, and he or she will look at you as though you had created some kind of abomination. Mexican salsas are complex, however, and can include up to twenty or so ingredients. The ingredients tend to reflect the landscape from both the past and the post-European culinary and agricultural introductions: cumin, tomato, cilantro, onion, garlic, varieties of both domesticated and wild chilis, Mexican oregano, and so on. Preparation and presentation vary as well. My Aunt Vera's salsa is more of what would be referred to as pico de gallo, whereby the ingredients are visibly discernible in the somewhat chunky sauce, yet the salsa lends itself to dipping with large homemade tortilla chips. However, many salsas found in Sonora are liquid styled and deeply flavored with cumins, paprikas, and several varieties of dried, fresh, and smoked chilis. There seems to be as many versions of Sonoran-styled salsas as there are families that conjure them up in their kitchens.

Our Seri hosts, like other Sonorenses, enjoyed their salsa *picante*. Unfortunately, the tradition of subsisting off their abundant Sonoran Desert landscape is disappearing as quickly as the green leatherback sea turtle they sing to in the Sea of Cortez. As a result, they primarily use the watery stuff enclosed in ill-capped glass bottles they can purchase in Mexican markets. The only handmade Sonoran-styled salsas we had the opportunity to partake of were the ones in the little *taquerías* we stopped at for lunch and dinner on our drive past Hermosillo, through Kino Bay, and finally into Desemboque.

We met Laurie in Kino Bay, quickly caught up, and then began our trek north into Seri country. Laurie led the way in her questionable old economy-sized pickup truck; we made toward Desemboque. The drive north from Kino Bay is relaxing if one is able to focus the mind on the surreal-teal sea waters on the left and the Sonoran Desert landscape on the passenger side of the relatively smooth dirt road that seems to keep the desert from encroaching onto the waters. Islands seem to float on the restless waters of the sea, while jagged ridges and peaks add backdrop to the cacti and prickly desert flora. It was difficult, however, to keep from wondering about the numerous "what would happen" scenarios. What would happen if the gas tank were punctured by a sharp rock, and we ran out of gas on this desolate landscape in 110-degree heat? What about if there were drug cartel bandits on the road? What if we got a flat, and then the spare went flat? Amid all the questions, the desert and the sea continue on past the windows with little care for our list of what-ifs.

I believe Celia noticed it first. It's difficult to recall, but the road reached a short rise where our view was slightly above the landscape ahead. A shoulder of desert seemed to extend roundly into the sea. Celia was looking at the shoulder and asked, "Is that it?" Just then, a truck came barreling toward us from the opposite direction, leaving its dust tail in its wake. Desemboque arises from the desert at the very last moment at the bend in the road. The small community of several hundred Seri and one Russian resembles one of those defunct housing developments one sees popping up at the edge of Southwestern cities and larger towns. Bulldozers move in first and dig out the frame of the neighborhood grids and roads, but then the promised residents buy up the lots and the planned neighborhoods never get off the ground. Finally, when the developers get desperate and lower the price of the lots, people purchase them and build whatever kind of structures they feel like, with little regard for housing codes. That is the current feel of Desemboque. The variety of structures sits on a grid much like that of an American town. This is strange to me because so much of Seri culture and history is non-Western and nonlinear. This is a culture that accepts spiritual people who sing to ocean currents and whose language includes identifying terms such as "what sea turtles throw up" for names of over 400 useful plants.

We made our way into the grid to where Gary and Laurie were staying. For some reason, we got to the house a little before Laurie did. The community was quiet. We got out of our air-conditioned vehicle and began to wilt in the heat and also from the humidity loitering in the air. The seawaters were 100 yards away, but did little to cool the air. In no time, people began to peer out of their homes, wondering who these strangers were hanging around at Gary and Laurie's place. Amalia was the first to venture over, into the shade of the large acacia tree where we were still assessing the situation. She greeted us warily, but in little time produced from a fold in her clothing about 10 strands of colorful and texturally unique necklaces constructed from small seashells. We showed some interest in the necklaces, which was a mistake. Soon, other woman wrapped in colorful printed cottons shawls and long skirts emerged around us like a swarm vying for attention to their necklaces, ironwood carvings, and baskets. Then, there were about twenty people milling about in front of Laurie's house. She soon showed up to help bring a bit of order to the melee, but it did not really calm down until an older gentleman began making his way into the crowd.

Everyone noticed him about the same time and sort of parted the way for him as he made his way toward us. I recognized Efrain in his bright turquoise-colored shirt in contrast to his dark skin. He was walking slowly and with the help of a couple of younger Seri. There was a big smile on his face, but also something different about him that had not been there the first time I met him up north in Arizona. When he found me with his eyes and quickened his step, that is when I realized what was new about him; he could see. And his smile broadened as he realized that it was me that he was looking at for the first time. As in disbelief, he said, "Enrique!?" We greeted each other as if we were long-lost friends. Everyone looked on equally pleased and excited by the encounter. We sat down in a couple of old, rusting lawn chairs and caught up as the rest of the community looked on, conversed, and sold necklaces to Celia and Laurie. I pulled up my laptop computer and showed photos of Efrain that I had taken when we had met earlier on the Hopi reservation. He was equally amazed at the technology as he was at the digital photos. In little time, however, he brought the conversation around to his songs: the songs about the stars, the songs that he wished for me to learn. In preparation for my visit, he had made a cassette tape of himself singing the songs. He produced the tape and handed it to me. In little time, he was singing the songs accompanied by the rhythm of clapping hand and stomping feet. Song is at the core of Seri resilience.

When I had originally met Efrain and his traveling companions on the Hopi mesas, it was immediately apparent that song was central to Seri way of being. They sat at a table in the restaurant on Hopi's Second Mesa and sang about their visit. Much to the surprise of the many Hopi and Navajo in the diners, who are normally a bit more reserved among strangers, the Seri sang about the food, about their homeland, and about the Sea of Cortez from which much of their worldview emerges. Back home in Mexico, Efrain, Amalia, Arturo, Gabriel, and most everyone young and old continue to practice the tradition of singing. They sing to ask the sea turtles to rise to the surface of the churning waters of the Sea of Cortez. They depend on the waters as a part of their subsistence; therefore, they sing to the unpredictable ocean currents as well as to the winds that can impair or sometimes aid their fishing. As one sees in many societies around the world that have maintained their cultural and community kincentric relationship to place, singing is more than a pastime or a source of entertainment. Encoded in the songs, sometimes cryptically and often readily apparent, are libraries of traditional ecological knowledge. In the case of the Seri, their songs reveal intimate observations of local sea life, plants, lifeways, and behaviors of mammals, plants, and amphibians. The songs reflect several layers of Seri worldview and cognition, because more

Figure 8.2 Seri musician El Indio, Punta Chueca, Sonora, Mexico.

than libraries of specific knowledge, the songs are refugia for Seri morals, values, and how to be Seri.

Seri being-ness is central to being Seri. The Native writer and poet N. Scott Momaday wrote in the preface of his collection of poems, *In the Presence of the Sun*, "Words are names. To write a poem is to practice a naming ceremony. . . . And [*sic*] to confer a name is to confer being." Being Seri is more than existing as a biological animal along the Sea of Cortez or within the confines of a modern Mexican grocery store in Hermosillo. Being Seri involves the act of perceiving the world in certain words: the words carefully archived by people such as Efrain and now, in a less traditional manner, by emerging Seri rock stars.

Resilience in a Rock Band's Lyrics

"You have to meet El Indio," Laurie told me when we first caught up in Kino Bay toward the beginning of this trip into Seri country. I thought the tag of "El Indio" a bit odd because everyone that we would be coming in contact with once we got into Seri country would be indigenous and, therefore, indios. The thought dashed through my mind that perhaps El Indio was somehow more indio than the rest. Apparently, El Indio was some sort of musician. Laurie knew that I was interested in traditional music and sounds and, more particularly, out to find ways to support traditional music that was a reflection of people's expressions of their relationship to place.

On the way to Desemboque, we had stopped in another Seri community named Punta Chueca. Today, most Seri live in either Desemboque or Punta Chueca. There was a group of Seri folks in Punta Chueca that Laurie wanted me to meet. I had funded a mapping project that they were engaged in. We pulled into the community in front of one of the more modern-looking buildings. Several Seri woman selling their necklaces, carvings, and basketry descended upon us. It is so difficult not to purchase anything because items such as the necklaces sell for about the equivalent of $1.50 each and are worth much more in terms of the time it takes to make one. The only drawback to showing interest in one artist's wares is that the others tend to swarm you in hopes that you may also purchase something of theirs. I had made the mistake of showing interest in a particularly well-woven basket and soon was surrounded by baskets, stone carvings, and colorful shell necklaces.

After the shopping spree, we were introduced to the local elders, who quickly arranged a demonstration of their traditional dance and song. Two singers adorned in colorful ribbon shirts sang accompanied by violin, hand drum, and flute. A line dance was performed by some of the younger women, and then young men slid a thick piece of plywood attached to a two-by-four frame into the center of the dance area. The music increased in speed while the dancers took turns dancing on the plywood that now acted as a sort of resonator for the dancers' stomp-style dance. Their footwork was very fast and intricate. As they took turns on the board, it appeared that they were also competing for who could be the fastest and most stylish. I was reminded of break-dancers north of the border who would pull sheets of thick cardboard onto a street or sidewalk and take turns out-posing each other. The performance lasted about 45 minutes. The elders still wanted to show off the incredible series of geographic information system (GIS) maps that they had available.

The maps were the result of years of working with local anthropologists, GIS experts, and ecologists as a part of a cultural mapping project. With the new maps, the Seri could demonstrate and reclaim in Mexican and international courts their traditional rights to fishing, coastal, and other territories. While we were reviewing the maps, I took a break from the hot and stuffy room where the maps where housed and stepped outside. Standing there near an open window was a tall and slender Seri with rather long, black, and very straight hair. He wore only a dark tank top, shorts, and sunglasses. He was a striking figure accentuated by the numerous tattoos adorning parts of his body. I noticed him admiring the intricate Maori-style tattoo on my left calf. In the ensuing conversation, we got around to talking about music. I often travel with a guitar. On this trip, I had brought along a very special acoustic Gibson guitar. We moved around to the back of my SUV so that he could strum the instrument. He seemed pleased with the sound and action of my guitar. This person eventually told me that he had a rock band he called *El Fuego Divino*, The Divine Fire. At that moment, I knew I had met El Indio. I asked his name, which was actually Francisco Molina.

As we discussed his music, he pulled a cassette tape from a pocket in his shorts and suggested that we listen to it. Fortunately, the SUV I was driving had a cassette player installed. We popped in the tape and cranked up the sound. El Fuego Divino's sound can best be described as heavy-punky-Seri-metal. The lyrics were all in Seri, but not really original. According to El Indio, the songs were mostly ancient Seri songs and poetry set against the rock sound. I was both impressed and excited. I knew that I had to find a way to support El Indio's sound. It turned out that the only available recording of El Fuego Divino's sound was that single cassette tape.

The GIS work was impressive and important. The process of recalling fishing areas and places that are sacred works to remind and solidify a community's connection and claims to a landscape. Before books, the Internet, and other forms of mass media, people reactivated these connections through song and oratory. El Indio and his band were updating Seri songs and making the sound applicable to today's young Seri ears.

On a subsequent visit to Punta Chueca, I had the opportunity to hear El Fuego Divino live. I had traveled to the area with the director of The Christensen Fund, Ken Wilson. We arrived at Punta Chueca during a very warm and quiet afternoon. I asked around for where El Indio lived and was led to one of the small stucco and wood houses at the back end of the village, nearest the waters of the Sea of Cortez. In the distance, Tiburon Island rose from the water. Its jagged and desert scrub–covered ridges and peaks backlit by the bright sun stood in contrast to the deep blue skies. In customary Mexican Indian fashion, we stood in front of the house until someone noticed we were there and came out to see what we were about. We asked about El Indio. The young man that greeted us mentioned that he had just returned from a hunt on Tiburon Island. El Indio emerged from the house into the sun dressed in camouflage and looking a bit tired. He told us about the hunt. He had not taken a bighorn sheep as he had hoped. He also said something in the ensuing conversation that remains with me. He said that at the beginning of the hunt one's ego is tall and strong. By the end, one's ego has shrunk. I believe El Indio's bit of humble philosophy stuck because it is a reflection of traditional values that recognize an individual's identity as one that is part of a larger whole and of a larger natural process. His songs reflect this understanding as well. The next day, El Fuego Divino was rehearsing in a sweltering metal building. The band members sat on barrels and boxes while playing. An audience of many young people, mostly between the ages of 9 and 14, sat and moved to the distorted bass and guitar and to El Indio's harmonic vocalizations. It was this scene that I had come to witness. El Fuego Divino drives to Hermosillo and other local communities to perform and make a few pesos. It is likely that the people in the audiences away from Punta Chueca have no idea what El Indio is singing about. They just enjoy the rock music and the excuse to dance. However, every time El Fuego Divino leaves to perform, it affords another opportunity for those young Seri to feel that their culture, their beliefs, and their identity are significant. In addition, when they sit there and move to El Fuego Divino's rehearsals, their deep sense of connection to the Sea of Cortez and to the desert landscape are reaffirmed and added to the long-term memory loop of resilience.

9

A New American Indian Cuisine

"DOES ANYONE KNOW how to start a fire?" she shouted. At first I thought the question a bit bizarre, considering we were standing outside, amid the juniper woods at the outskirts of Santa Fe, New Mexico. Surely people in this neck of the woods knew how to start a fire. Lois Ellen Frank was standing there in her chef whites in the late morning New Mexico sun, looking for anyone that would build and ignite a fire so that she and the other American Indian chefs could proceed with some over-the-fire cooking. Lois was co-coordinating a large food-related gathering and didn't have time to start the fire herself. After 48 years of pit roasting with my family, countless campfires, time spent in the military, and just being a kid, I knew a little something about starting cooking fires. I quickly volunteered and got to work.

Lois Ellen Frank, Loretta Oden, Walter Whitewater, and several other American Indian chefs, food activists, writers, academics, and food producers were part of a gathering sponsored partly by Slow Food USA's Renewing America's Food Traditions (RAFT) symposium at the Institute of American Indian Arts (IAIA) campus outside of Santa Fe.

This meeting was only one among several devoted to identifying producers across the country that are hanging on to or reviving foods and foodways that have been present in North America for the last several generations. Many of these food traditions are inevi-

Figure 9.1 Rarámuri squashes behind Gabriel Molina's home, Norogachi, Chihuahua, Mexico.

tably American Indian in origin, using ingredients native to North American landscapes. Lois and the others were present not only to participate in the day and a half of dialogue but also to offer up tastings of some of these foods. Some of the foods served included quinoa falafel, puffed quinoa, flourless chocolate torte, chili-honey glazed quail, cedar-planked salmon, and my personal favorite of the day, mole negro. I have always mentioned to anyone within earshot that mole is nearest to the type of intricate foods that Mesoamericans consumed when Europeans first floundered their way into North America. Mole is a complex dish fully representative of the landscape and agricultural system cultivated by Central Americans. The list of ingredients and the numerous steps involved in producing even a simple mole are multifaceted enough to cause any culinary student to pause. Why then, Lois Ellen Frank asks, are American Indian foods not considered a cuisine equal to that of French, Italian, and Asian?

Lois has made this question her mission, which has led to a colorful food-oriented book full of recipes and soon to her completed dissertation and PhD focusing on the subject. Some might regard the unique preparatory steps, agriculture, harvesting, and even eating, devoted to preparing foods such as corn, a cuisine unique to North America. In essence, this is cuisine. At one level, posole is simply a stew of corn, spices, and sometimes bits of meat, depending on the region and even the family that is preparing the dish. Approached with preparation in mind, posole requires a specified manner of first growing a certain type of corn hybridized over centuries to fit the tastes that Native people have come to appreciate in a bowl of posole. As a result, posole is also the kind of corn that is used in the preparation of the dish. The term activates a mental blend in the minds of people culturally familiar with this kind of food.

Posole preparation employs dried hominy corn that has had its hulls removed. The corn is soaked in water overnight. The next day, the corn is placed in a cooking pot that cannot be metal, or at least it must be an enameled pot. This requirement is essential to the process because the step involves the addition of culinary ash, which reacts negatively to metal. Culinary ash is the white ash left over from the complete burning of certain types of woods. Depending on the culture and on what foods are being prepared, the ash may be from saltbush, juniper, or even bean plants. The lye and alkali present in the ash have a way of making the niacin present in the corn available for the human digestive process and also change the corn's color and consistency. After boiling for about 5 hours, the hominy is cooled under running water while one's fingers work to remove the hulls. Next, the hominy is dried again and stored for later use. One can appreciate from this description that Native foods are beyond simple ones that are only raised, harvested, dried, and then eaten. These foods involve a process that reflects centuries of creativity and innovation. Another innovative and equally complex Southwestern food is piki bread.

Piki is one of North America's original breads. Prior to European contact, Native North America did not know sourdough, ciabatta, or even seven-grain flax/oatmeal breads. The nearest to bread-like foods were corn tortillas, tamales, and what the Hopi came to know as piki. Piki comes in newsprint-thin sheets of cooked batter rolled up and served at special occasions. Making piki requires both art and skill. Young Hopi brides must demonstrate their adeptness at making piki prior to being considered suitable to be married. Piki is "baked" in special piki houses on flat stones that have been seasoned. Piki stones become family treasures, handed down through several generations. The thick stone rests elevated above smaller stones normally at the edge or corner of a piki house. Cedar branches are burnt under the stone during the cooking process. The batter consists of water, normally blue cornmeal, and culinary ash. Sometimes yellow and white cornmeal is used, depending on the ceremonial purpose. The thin batter, the consistency of runny pancake batter, is spread on the stone with bare hands by the adept chef. I have never tried this process, but according to Jane, it takes years to master the technique while losing a few layers of fingertip skin. The batter is rubbed onto the stone in layers. When dried to the proper consistency, the layers are peeled off the stone into one sheet and then rolled up. After the cooking process, and while the stone remains hot, the stone is "greased" with ground-up watermelon or squash seeds. The natural oils from the seeds seep into the stone. Eating piki is an art in itself. One bite into the bread results in a shower of crumbs down the front of the eater. I have often had to surrender to my messiness as a piki eater or attempt to take small bites, which doesn't ever seem to result in fewer crumbs. I have also tried the dip and bite approach whereby one dips the end of the bread into a stew or sauce and then bites into it. The result is often the same, but it sure is fun.

When piki is served or is present on a table, the result is often many smiles and elevated conversation, especially from Hopi and other Pueblo peoples. Piki is one of those special occasion foods that transports people to moments in time captured in the memory and uploads by certain smells and sites. These stored moments are normally pleasant ones, often from childhood. Piki acts as mental refugia of cultural memory, cultural survival, and identity. Piki can even activate ecological knowledge related to agricultural techniques and wild crafting culinary ash. It is a spring of resilience that gushes forth when it is eaten. Piki can blend with other refugia foods, creating mosaics of cultural memory and resilience. Another such food that evokes a concert of cultural and sensual reaction from peoples from the Southwest and is also one of the simplest is roasted green chili.

Mention roasted green chili to any native, whether Hispano, indigenous, or Anglo, and then plan for reactions ranging from sheer ambrosia to disdain and a litany of stories and anecdotes from the funny and absurd to the soulful and spiritual.

Chili has become one of those identifier foods of the American Southwest, along with tortillas, tamales, and enchiladas. Historically, chili is not really a traditional food of the American Southwest. It was introduced to these regions when Spanish colonists began moving north from the Valley of Mexico during the sixteenth century. Chili's origins are farther south in places such as Bolivia, the highlands of Peru, the Tehuacan Valley of Mexico, and other tropical areas of Central and South America. The only variety of chili that existed in the Greater Southwest before its mass migration was the chiltepin, also known as *chili pequin*. This tiny red pepper in maturity grows erect on small bushes in the wild. The fruits are about the size of a one's pinky fingernail. My grandmother used to grow these tiny balls of fire in our field. She would grind about two of them up to add to a pot of beans or a stew. That was enough to change a bland pot of beans into a mouth-stimulating dish.

Chiltepins are highly respected in northwest Mexico to the point where unique chiltepin-grinding contraptions can be found on family dining tables. They are carved from ironwood in creative shapes and designs. The working part is a simple hole drilled into the top of the tool with a long plug resting in the hole. The plug has some teeth carved into its working end. As with other chilis, one has to be careful when handling chiltepins. An errant touch to one's lips, eyes, or nose can result in irritation for about an hour or so due to the irritant, capsaicin, found to varying degrees in all chilis. People in places such as Sonora, Mexico, however, like to crunch the small dried peppers into their meals. One way they have dealt with avoiding the irritation is to use the grinding contraption. The chiltepin is placed into the hole, the plug is placed in the hole on top of the pepper, and then it is twisted around for a couple of seconds. The plug is removed, and the ground pepper can now be safely poured onto one's foods.

With an insightful and creative touch, the RAFT movement identified what is largely the Greater Southwest as the Chile Pepper Nation. One cannot begin a catalog of most Southwestern meals and dishes without including chilis as either an ingredient or a condiment. The mildly irritating, addictive, and powerful spice is grown throughout the region by the hundreds of acres, in people's home gardens, and in pots resting on someone's apartment balcony in Albuquerque or Phoenix. Chili consumption, the ability to eat or not eat it, reaches deep levels of regional and cultural identity. Those considered "local" to the Southwest must be able to claim that they have at least tried to eat chili. Chili consumption varies by degrees of "hotness." Chilis are not really hot in terms of temperature, but feel hot due to the capsaicin level. Among some circles, the ability to eat chilis is a sign of manhood or strengthens one's claim to localness. In the Sierra Madres of Chihuahua, Mexico, many Tarahumara are wary of people that do not like or refuse to eat chili. People there feel that only evil sorcerers don't eat chili.

People become sensitive and sentimentally mystical about chili and chili-based remedies. I was talking with Emigdio Ballon, the spiritual farmer from Bolivia now raising foods for Tesuque Pueblo, and asked about whether he was growing chili. He was squatting and peering down toward the ground when I asked him this question in his greenhouse. From my vantage point, I could see his eyebrows snap up to attention. He cranked his neck to look up at me. His normally serious demeanor had shifted to one of faux incredulity, coupled with a knowing smirk that caused only one end of his mouth and face to form a partial smile. "Enrique," he said in his rich accented English. "I 'ave sumding for ju dat ju will loav." Later, when we returned to his office near the Tesuque Pueblo civil buildings, he produced a small bottle that at one time had contained an herbal beverage from China. The screw-on lid worked to keep a rubber stopper in place. Behind the clear glass, was an orange-red liquid. He carefully handed me the bottle, indicating that it was a precious gift. I motioned to open the bottle in order to smell what was inside. Emigdio quickly cautioned me to be careful with the contents of the bottle. I unscrewed the lid and then removed the rubber stopper. My sinuses and eyes were immediately assaulted, but at the same time pleasantly embraced by the liquid pungency of chili oil. Emigdio began chanting the many medical uses of the oil from treating cold and flu to being an antibiotic. I knew, however, what I was going to do with this ambrosia once I got it into my kitchen. The oil has since acted as a preventative medicine while, at the same time, enhancing the flavors of my home-cooked pinto beans, omelets, and tortilla soup.

Foods such as chili, piki bread, and posole are contemporary markers of our human legacy. They remind us of our continued efforts to blend past and present while we reach for a future wherein our communities maintain their cultural flavors and colors while we enhance the beauty of the landscapes with which we live and whose stewardship we have been bestowed with. The foods and dishes along which they are served and eaten are final products of processes that have dynamically reflected the human–land relationships across the Greater Southwest. Alex Sando of Jemez Pueblo (and now director of American Indian Outreach at Native Seeds/Search) expresses this concept more in terms of a current emanation of generations of Native people that have grown, processed, and eaten these foods. His voice is only one contemporary voice of centuries of Jemez people that have stewarded the land and its fruits. When people such as Lois, Eric, Miguel, and Juan till the land, they reflect a community that has been on that same land since our origin stories were first told. Today's chiltepin-crushing device—engraved with images of cactus, birds, and other nature-based icons—connects not only the past to the present but also the arid Southwestern landscape to the pot of posole simmering on Grandma's stove. The current relationship is at risk due to many internal and external pressures and changes. We no longer have the time to enhance the beauty of our places. In the past, before we burned fossil fuels, time was encamped in the land. When we began burning fossil fuels, we began to release the time embedded in the Earth. We began to decalibrate time created during the same period as the creation of the lands. How do we then regain the time that we increasingly are losing and wasting? According to Carlo Petrini, the founder of the Slow Food movement, we must eat slowly.

The RAFT gathering went very well. It was warm on the verge of being hot, and all of the first day's activities were outside. Many of the "Redskins" become Redskins due to lack of sunscreen. Everyone who is anyone in the RAFT movement was there. The founder of the concept, Gary Nabhan, reigned over his table of heritage foods. Winona LaDuke fielded countless questions and struggled to find time to relax with her beadwork. Potowanami chef and film documentarian Loretta Oden cooked and presented a short talk. Three young native chefs from the Santa Fe Community College Culinary Arts program helped Loretta and other Native foods chefs such as John Sharpe from La Posada in Winslow, Arizona, and Diné chef Walter Whitewater. Tomas Enos of the Institute of American Indian Arts, which hosted the event on its campus, hawked his wild-crafted herbal sunscreen, bug repellent, and beauty products, while Clayton Brascoupe and his family made and gave away piki bread and Tesuque-style blue corn tamales. Patty Martinson and Terry Badhand, codirectors of the Taos County Economic Development Corporation (TCEDC), sat at their table that revealed what their organization does. Miguel Santistevan brought many smiles and colorful stories wherever he was present on the grounds, and Emigdio Ballon impressed everyone with the culinary flexibility of quinoa. Melissa Nelson, Laura Baldez, Nicola Waldberg, Bernadette Zambrano, and Ann Marie Sayers of The Cultural Conservancy occupied a display table of their *Salt Song Trail* DVDs and conducted numerous recorded oral histories related to foodways.

This meeting reflected another significant marker very few people outside of this secluded world recognize. Thirty years ago, a list of Native food producers could fit on a 3" × 5" index card. Today, a handful of books, pamphlets, and recent RAFT publications are continuing to update the growing resurgence of Native food producers sprouting up across North America. The sprouts include wild rice producers from Minnesota, a bison rancher in South Dakota, a Navajo family in nearby Teec Nos Pos, Arizona, offering Churro sheep, and a Pueblo foods specialist in Albuquerque. The list is extensive and growing. The resurgence of traditional Native foodways also is an expression of a revitalization of cultural identity and practice. One of my favorite examples of this revitalization of cultural practice is TCEDC's mobile Matanza billed, in its simple threefold pamphlet with a color photo on the front of the eighteen-wheeled mobile unit, as "New Mexico's First Mobile Livestock Slaughtering Unit . . . Providing Quality Livestock Slaughtering & Cut & Wrap Services for Northern New Mexico."

Up until just before World War II, most of rural northern New

Mexico was economically self-sustaining. Native and Hispano agriculturalists grew and raised most of what they ate. There was even a variety of wheat grown in the region, which has somehow survived on the fields of only two remaining Hispano farmers. Unfortunately, growing Taos Red wheat is more of a hobby rather than a sustainable practice because the nearest mill is nearly 500 miles away. Old-timers flash nostalgic when they describe how the northern New Mexican town of Questa used to have its own mill. In a similar fashion, small-scale livestock raisers hanging on to varieties of sheep, goats, and beef have been in decline due to the difficulty and economic strain related to getting their meat USDA inspected, slaughtered, and packed. As these farmers and their animals dissolve into nonexistence, so do the remaining varieties of livestock, which may maintain genetic and hardy resistance to the growing mutations of farmland pests, parasites, and diseases inundating current food breeds and herds. Maintaining breeds such as those in places like northern New Mexico present the possibility of freeing current agriculturalists from chemical dependency. Enter center stage TCEDC's mobile Matanza.

It was no place for a vegetarian. Fortunately, I am an omnivore. Terry, Patty, and their new Matanza driver led me out the back door of TCEDC's offices to where the eighteen-wheeled slaughtering unit sat. Its tires were partially embedded in the deep remnants of northern New Mexico's recent blizzard and quickly rising mud. Based on their large smiles and lifted voices, one would think that they were introducing me to a newborn baby. Their optimism and exuberance were contagious. The recently hired driver for the mobile unit was equally excited as he slung open the large rear doors of the attached trailer. The unit was lined with stainless steel sinks, and other stainless contraptions I was at a loss to distinguish uses for were attached to the walls of the trailer. Large meat hooks hung from the ceiling. I immediately imagined animal carcasses of various types hanging from the ceiling. There was a side door toward the back of the mobile room where the wastes are pushed out. I was just as excited for TCEDC as they all were.

The unit represents, in an agricultural and mostly cultural way, a rebirth of sorts in the community. Small-scale agriculture in New Mexico is indicative of agriculture in the region. Due to geographical, historical, and cultural limitations, small isolated fields tucked away in lush stream-fed *rincóns* and narrow valleys have been the legacy for nearly 400 years. In addition, small herds of sheep, goats, and cattle roamed the commonly managed mountainsides and green river bottoms. This kind of agriculture flourished for so long for the same geographical and cultural reasons and in a market that sustained it. Gentrification has changed the local economy and has threatened the very sustainable forces that have enhanced the beauty of the Land of Enchantment. Land values, privatization, and Bureau of Land Management (BLM) and Forest Service land use regulations have worked also to send local agricultural interests into decline, mostly because people simply cannot afford it.

Ernie Atencio knows the impacts of local traditional agricultural decline intimately. He is the director of the Taos Land Trust (TLT). His small organization has worked steadfastly to plug the drain of small-scale local agricultural lands and the people that steward them. The TLT accomplishes this Herculean task through helping Hispano and Native families arrange land trust and conservation easements that allow the landowner to feel the comfort of being able to transfer ownership of family-held lands without the fear of the next generation having to sell the land due to rising taxes.

Ernie drove me around the area just north and east of Taos in his Subaru wagon, which had obviously bounced across hundreds of miles of New Mexico's enchanted, but washboarded and dusty roads. We were on a tour to view some of the TLT's work. The landscape outside Taos is the southern end of an intermontane basin that begins north in Colorado. Taos itself rests at about 8,000 feet in elevation. The basin floor is abutted to the east by the Sangre de Cristo Mountains. The flat land slopes away from the mountains toward the west, interrupted only by the Rio Grande Gorge. Most of the land is set aside for grazing; but closer to Taos and the other small villages of Arroyo Seco, Arroyo Hondo, and Pilar, pastures of primarily alfalfa abound, separated by old wire fences held up by even older juniper posts. Ernie seemed to know the owner and history of each parcel. He pointed out where their acequias lay on the edges of their fields. He retold the story of families that were forced to stop growing food crops replacing them with alfalfa for animals, but who still managed to grow heirloom apples. Ernie knew these stories not only as a result of his work but also because his legacy and that of his family were rooted in this landscape of sagebrush and junipers. When he spoke of northern New Mexico red chili, his voice reflected others whose identities breathe this particular land and the foods that it can give life to. The others are not only Ernie's contemporaries but also those generations that stewarded this land during the previous eras. This is why people such as Ernie, Miguel Santistevan, Juan Estevan Arellano, Clayton Brascoupe, Emigdio Ballon, and Paula Garcia begin to protest and then act when the sovereignty of their foods is threatened.

It's not just about the food. The food that reaches the table is the final product of a process that is currently threatened. In this case, the food and food choices have become political symbols, revealing struggles for self-determination in places such as New Mexico. Eating a bowl of posole made from locally grown corn, lamb, and chili is equal to going to the state legislature to demand fair water rights. This is because when one either grows one's own ingredients for the posole or barters or purchases the foods from someone who did, one is supporting a resilient process aimed at sovereignty. Through the Greater Southwest's struggles for water rights, access to commonly managed grazing lands, recognition of historic land grants, protection from overzealous development, and the limiting of GMO foods raised in the area are growing in intensity and threatening the livelihoods, land-based traditions, and cultural vitality of indigenous communities. As an act of protest, several small-scale farmers held a meeting at Tesuque Pueblo. One result was a Declaration of Seed Sovereignty.

Local organizations such as the Traditional Native American Farmers Association, the New Mexico Acequia Association, the Taos Valley Acequia Association, and local Pueblo communities have struggled for the land and water rights for decades. The struggle was difficult, but appeared eventually to be winnable. The various associations were aware of each other's struggles because they mirrored each other. Often, they banded together for particular legislative reforms or to try fight new laws and regulations. The fight was good and obvious because it was tactile. Fighting for water and land is real. One can touch and eventually walk on it or eat it, but something new entered the fray, which wasn't so tactile. Industrial agriculture came to New Mexico a generation ago and began the process of concentrating food production to fewer people and into places distant from the people that would eat the foods. Industrial agriculture also brought the threat of genetically modified organisms (GMOs). Pollen from GMO chili can travel on the winds, touch on Miguel Santistevan's chili plants, interbreed with them, and therefore sever the legacy of his heirloom plants and those of others. Pollen is not so tactile. I recall bringing up this topic with Juan Estevan Arellano as we sat in the open kitchen in his home in Embudo. He looked down at the dinner table where we were sitting when he pondered the question of GMOs. Finally, he looked up and sadly asked, "How do we fight the wind?" Yet, a movement has begun in New Mexico that is already spreading. The New Mexico Acequia Association and the Traditional Native American Farmers Association joined forces to adopt the Declaration dated March 11, 2006. Its opening lines express the overall theme of the movement: "to continue, revive, and protect our native seeds, crops, heritage fruits, animals, wild plants, traditions and knowledge of our indigenous land and acequia-based communities in New Mexico for the purpose of maintaining and continuing our cultural integrity and resisting the global industrialized food system that can corrupt our lives, freedom and culture through inappropriate food production and genetic engineering." The Declaration was one result of a Traditional Agriculture Conference held March 10–11, 2006, in Alcalde, New Mexico. A seed exchange ceremony took place at the beginning of the meeting as a way to declare the interconnectedness of the participants. After the Declaration was released, the Eight Northern Indian Pueblos Council, the All Indian Pueblo Council, as well as the National Congress of American Indians got wind of it and endorsed it. In little time, the counties of Santa Fe and Rio Arriba adopted the Declaration, and the State of New Mexico is currently considering adoption with some rewording. The beauty and strength of this document is not so much in its wording, but more that it was composed by the very people whose lifestyles, culture, identity, and belief system are at risk. These people represent a segment of our population that understands not only humanity's role in maintaining biocultural diversity but also that further industrialization of our food systems and the people that rely on them present a great risk to our future human legacy.

Food sovereignty for Native peoples is the antithesis to the industrialization of all people. When a Navajo child is born, the grandparents give the child a lamb. That child's role now is to raise that lamb to become a source of wool and perhaps food. From that early gift, a Navajo child learns the responsibility of connecting with an animal and, as a result, the land. Sustainable stewardship and cultural resilience are neither decisions nor rights. Nowhere in the Declaration of Seed Sovereignty does the notion of term of rights arise. Instead, the associations conferred to include in their "living document" concepts of relationships, generational memory, embodied practices, spirituality, caring, respect, traditions, and celebration when declaring their revival and survival of their way of life. Together, these concepts reflect identity connected to responsibility toward one's place in a community within a landscape. Responsibility implies that one considers first the land, and others, and future generations before acting. As a result, humanity's food future is a responsibility not only for us but also for the land.

Renewing America's Food Traditions (RAFT) is not about preserving an heirloom tomato that can be purchased for an outlandish price at swanky farmer's markets, but about renewing whole traditions related to indigenous lifestyles that are connected to food. It is often the case, however, that these foods are the ones grown in a place for generations. Together with restaurant owners, food distributors, and the traditional food producers, RAFT is forging a path that will revive traditional farming lifestyles, the foods raised on these lands, and the sustainable stewardship that has accompanied the whole system. In the Americas, we are talking about Churro sheep formerly raised by Navajo herdsmen throughout the reservation, but now reduced to only a handful of families. The process will include farmers throughout North America whose families have brought foods to their and their community's tables. Makah fishermen off the coast of the Pacific Northwest are not left out. They reflect community-wide efforts to restore what once was a thriving and sustainable fishing lifestyle, which not only harvested whales but also acted to enhance the whale population. In the same

manner, abalone gatherers off the coast of California have seen abalone populations dwindle to near nothing as a result of overharvesting and are working to reverse this trend. These and other activists
act as stewards of their communities and are collaborating with
RAFT to host regional in situ workshops, which first are identifying
foods and food producers that are at risk. They then are attending
larger regional meetings at which solutions to how to turn trends
around are discussed. Here, the community stewards work across a
broad spectrum of farmers, fishermen, livestock raisers, chefs, consumers, and producer groups. This work is crucial. Through the
local workshops, many foods have been identified as near extinct. A
species of abalone reduced to a population of 1,500 was identified
and preserved; a variety of corn grown by only three farmers is another example.

As much as RAFT is about preserving lifestyles connected to
foodways, it is equally about promoting a cuisine. At the RAFT
meeting in Santa Fe, Lois had intentionally invited the three young
Native chefs from the Santa Fe Community College Culinary Arts
program to act as sous chefs for the other professional Native chefs.
These three young men helped Lois, Walter, Loretta, and the others prepare the ancestral-based foods. Most of these foods included
ingredients the young chefs had never worked with, let alone tasted,
before. That day's presentation included not only practical cooking
tips and lessons but also exposed the young chefs to an alternative
approach to foods connected to their own heritage. In addition,
their culinary teacher at Santa Fe Community College is promoting
Native cuisine in the classroom. What better value to offer young
professionals than one that reminds them that their cultural values
are significant in the world into which they are preparing to enter.

Promoting ancestral foodways makes economic and ecological
sense. Currently, the foods that reach the refrigerators and home-
cooked meals of Americans are transported over 1,500 miles to the
final destination, whether it is a grocery store or someone's backyard barbeque. Often, depending on the part of the nation, the
foods travel over 2,000 miles from production source to final
cooked meal. To large agribusiness board rooms, the current situation makes bottom-line sense: grow the most foods per acre, using
chemical fertilizers and pesticides, as long as the companies can

continue to be subsidized by the US government. When this cannot happen, they have moved their operations to Third World countries, where they can raise foods at the lowest price possible using cheap labor and relaxed environmental regulations. Economically speaking, however, this approach does little for the small-scale farmer trying to eke out a living in southern Mexico, Chile, or Brazil. Where the local economy is frail, the farmer's neighbors will choose to buy their cornmeal from the local grocer who is offering agribusiness-grown corn at a fraction of what it takes the local guy to bring his corn from field to market.

It is becoming increasingly obvious to researchers that the promise of GMO crops has fallen short. More people are starving today or going to bed hungry than at any time in the past, despite the increase in genetically modified foods and large-scale agribusiness subsidized by the World Bank, the International Monetary Fund, and the United Nations (UN). Foods grown in the backyards of people starving in the Third World are immediately shipped to the Whole Foods grocery stores in neighborhoods of Americans and Europeans that can afford the increasingly expensive shipping costs. But increases in the price of oil are causing even some Costco outlets to limit the number of bags customers can take from the store. In the ecological sense, this system is not logical.

GMOs and large-scale agribusiness decrease soil productivity as a result of farmers having to use Monsanto-based fertilizers that drain the microorganisms from once fertile lands. On top of that, many GMO plants are designed to release toxins for specific pests, which would decrease the harvest. Unfortunately, the toxins also tend to harm beneficial pollinating and other insects that are good for the overall health of the ecosystems that border the farmlands. Our quest for more foods is actually acting to decrease what the land can produce. Petroleum-based fertilizers damage soils, local plants, animals, and insects; seep into the water table; and now are threatened by the rising costs of crude oil. So much of our food cycle is dependent on these fertilizers that, without them, farmers will be at a loss of how to keep up with the rising demand for food. The economic and ecologic viability of our foods are on the verge of collapse. Food resilience declined even more each time a local farm was sold for a housing development, each time a family farm went out of business, and each time Papa was forced to begin using GMO-related seed and fertilizers.

Cultural changes are inevitable in any society. In fact, change should be included as part of the definition of culture. Culture is ever changing as communities and populations of people adapt and shift to both internal and external forces. For the most part, the specific changes are not subject to polarized judgment: whether or not it is good or bad for the community or culture. Change is simply part of the dynamic of any given society. It's a bit more difficult to accept, however, when the changes are reflected in individuals with whom one has grown up. It was mentioned earlier in this book that my family and I ate lots of traditional foods. We celebrated them at family gatherings and holidays. Because we were of a relatively lower income status, many of these foods comprised much of our daily diets. For the most part, I never gave the foods much thought beyond the fact that they were good and that I couldn't wait until my grandma made those cinnamon *bisqochitos* again or my Uncle Ray made menudo. I knew that our foods were different from those that the nonnative kids ate at school. It was also a special treat when those times arose that we could go to a fast-food joint or even to a Chinese restaurant.

The impact of changes socked me into a short lived and shallow depression recently when I went to a family gathering. Attending the gathering were many extended family members that I had not seen for quite a while. Many I had not seen for over 20 years. My time spent away from this part of my family was accentuated, as I had to constantly consult my mom and one of my closer aunts as to who was who throughout the afternoon. I was in disbelief when it was revealed to me that one of the many obese family members was someone that I had thought of as "hot" when I was a younger man. I had made it a part of my academic career to point out and discuss obesity and nutrition-related health disparities in other communities, but had not looked to my own family as an example.

When David Kozak conducted his psychological study of the Pima Indians suffering from diabetes on the Gila River reservation just south of Phoenix, he reported that the people were aware of their disease and, to a degree, had knowledge of it and even access to educational literature and programs that might prove to help them prevent the debilitating disease. However, Kozak's interview data continued to return him to the realization that so many of the respondents had "surrendered" themselves to getting diabetes. They assumed that, because they were Pima and that so much of the Pima population (50 percent of adults over the age of 35 at the time of the study) suffered and were dying from diabetes, they could do little to prevent it. I couldn't help wondering whether many of my cousins, second cousins, aunts, and uncles were making similar assumptions. At the family gatherings, the "traditional" foods made their appearance. Once the tamales hit the serving tables, the party was official. We savored the carne asada, and our mouths watered over the fresh-made corn tortillas. It was as though no one ate these foods anymore.

In any society, when something becomes rare but remains a significant part of the culture, it attains the status of icon. It becomes a symbol of something other than its original purpose. In this case, corn tortillas that were once consumed on a daily basis at nearly every meal have become a reminder of our Indian and Mexicanness. Flour tortillas are easier to attain and last longer in the refrigerator. Danishes and high-sugar cereals have replaced corn tortillas and beans for breakfast, a bean burrito in the lunch box has been replaced with a hamburger and fries, and home-cooked meals with the family have become compartmentalized in between soccer practice, dance class, and reality TV. The closest anyone comes to farming or managing the landscape is the maintenance of small family gardens and trying to keep the city from chopping down the stand of prickly pear cactus in the vacant lot on the other side of the fence. Within a generation, a group of people that were once part of a larger and extended population that maintained the landscape are now a tiny segment of a very large population that gets most of its food from 1,500 miles away, eats a high fat high sugar diet, is obese, is dying from what is eaten, and no longer maintains a connection to place. We no longer eat our landscape, but the landscapes of others. Responsibility for and protection of the other's land is not required.

10

The Whole Enchilada

I AM A MEMBER of a small group of fortunate scholars, writers, activists, meditation instructors, and nonprofit leaders that comprises the faculty for the Center for Whole Communities mentioned earlier in the book. For the last seven years, the faculty has been meeting separately to dialogue about the Center's curriculum and to plan for the following round of retreats. Six years ago, we met in Jackson Hole, Wyoming, nestled among the pines in a small log building at the Murie Center's small campus along the Snake River at the foot of the stunning Teton Mountains. This log building is the very place where the Wilderness Act was composed, which was later signed into existence in 1964. This important piece of legislation has done a great deal to help protect our wild places, dwindling population of species, habitats, and remaining open spaces. At one point during the faculty retreat, we were trying to figure out whether the Center for Whole Communities required a new name. All sorts of possibilities emerged, most of which incorporated the word whole. At one point, Helen, Peter's wife, suggested the phrase "whole enchilada" as a way to tell what the Center is all about; it's about including everything in how we approach environmental justice, social justice, ecological protection, economic concerns, and all the rest of the human and natural world issues that are being attacked, threatened, and oppressed. This final chapter is about this notion. The best way for me to help you get there is to evoke, once again, the lessons from my Rarámuri heritage.

Figure 10.1 Rarámuri children at El Mirador, Divisadero, Chihuahua, Mexico.

It was demonstrated previously that to the Rarámuri the natural world is not one of wonder, but of familiarity. We maintain this kincentric relationship to everything around us. It is a world in which the human niche is only one of a myriad of united niches that work together to continue the process of *iwígara*: the interconnectedness and cycling of all there is. If one aspect of the lasso is removed, the integrity of the circle is threatened, and all other aspects are weakened. In *iwígara*, all is bound, connected, and affected by a sharing breath.

The human mind verbalizes only that which it has experienced. This suggests that when our inner self begins its journey, it "awakens" into a world that we eventually come to reflect. Experiences become knowledge, both of which depend on being in a world that is inseparable from our bodies, our language, and our social history. Francisco Varela would come to call this phenomenon embodied cognition. David Abram simplified a description of the phenomenon when he wrote in *The Spell of the Sensuous* that "we are human only in contact, and conviviality, with what is not human." Humans enter the world uniquely "tuned for relationships" and able to express them verbally. If Abram and Varela are correct, then American Indian cultural models of the land and of the natural world are reflections of our centuries of experience with our places. For the Rarámuri, the experiences are developed in the model of *iwígara*.

The fragrance of certain flowers is believed to carry the soul of plants. In a *yúmari* song, the singer thanks a lily for allowing him to smell its scent, therefore providing him with strength. So we find also a Rarámuri notion of health related to flower scents and breath. When the women dance at *yúmari*, they symbolize the reproductive and fertile parts of the flower and therefore its life-giving breath. Suwi-ki, the corn beer, is consumed at every ritual and ceremony. But before it is consumed, the corn kernels, from which it is brewed, must be brought to life. The sprouting and fermentation stages of the brewing process are crucial because this is when the breath of the corn is released, affording life to the brew. When the corn beer is consumed, so is the breath of the corn.

The physical application of *iwígara* is at the heart of Rarámuri land management philosophy. Iwígara becomes most clear with regard to managing the land. It is *iwígara* that guides agriculture, medicine, and foraging. The use of plants for healing and for food offers a foundational relationship from which the Rarámuri view themselves as participants in their natural community. The Rarámuri perceive the land as a relative that must be cared for and nurtured. Rarámuri cultural history tells how the people emerged into this world from ears of corn. Another version tells that the people were put on the land by the Creator with corn in their ears. Both versions show that the Rarámuri understand that they are a part of the land, that they were placed here as caretakers of their land, and that they are directly responsible for the health of the Creator, who works hard each day to provide for the land and its inhabitants.

My friend and mentor, Jesusita, and her granddaughter Carolina often collected edible greens but, their collecting trips were neither special fractions of time, nor specifically planned. They collected plants as they came over to visit, or during in-between times when they enjoyed stopping by the creek to toss rocks into the water. I once came upon Jesusita and her shadow (this is how I thought of

Carolina) at the creek. They were laughing, enjoying the splashes their efforts were producing. The 66 years of Jesusita's life seemed to have never happened. I asked, "What are you doing?" Jesusita said, "Just throwing." Jesusita's knowledge of the use of the plants in her mountains was not just a stored collection of facts, recipes, and illness. Instead, it was a result of a lifelong relationship she had cultivated with her home. Her granddaughter's relationship has long since sprouted and is growing strongly.

When Jesusita spoke of the land, the religious and romantic overtones so prevalent in Western environmental conversation were absent. To her, the land existed in the same manner as did her family, her chickens, the river, and the sky. No hierarchy of privilege placed one above or below another. To Jesusita, *iwígara* bound and managed the interconnectedness of all life. Within this web, there were particular ways that living things related to one another. All individual life played a role in the cycle. She once said, "It is the reason why people should collect plants in the same way that fish should breathe water, and birds eat seeds and bugs. These are things we are supposed to do."

When discussing plant collecting, Jesusita became cautious and reminded me that collecting plants was done only at certain times and in certain places. This was so as not to disturb or offend the plants or the places in which the plants grew. Jesusita preferred to collect her long jack pine needles, which she used for basket weaving, at only a handful of places, all a half day's walk from her community. In this way, she prevented overharvesting of the needles and maintained a relationship with all the directions from her home.

Rarámuri women use several other natural materials for weaving. *Sereke* (*Dasylirion simplex*), *sokó* (*Yucca decipiens*), and *ruyá* (*Nolina matapensis*) comprise the three most widely used basket materials, along with pine needles. There has been a large tourist demand for Rarámuri baskets since the Chihuahua-Pacifico Railroad opened the region to tourism in the 1960s. They are sold on a daily basis along the railway, in the numerous gift shops in the region, and to the traders who ship them by railcar load to the United States. It would seem that overharvesting of weaving materials might be a risk. Yet the materials, found in the pine forests and along the walls of the barrancas, are carefully managed. This is due largely to the collection philosophy expressed by Jesusita. Traditional harvesting of these basket-making materials is periodic. Only the older leaves are collected. This process helps to sustain the health of the plants. The scientific explanation might be that the process suppresses sexual reproduction of the plants and promotes vegetative regrowth.

Overharvesting is an enduring concern in the Sierra Tarahumara, where arable land is cherished and the pressures of logging and narcotics trafficking are making sustainable horticulture uncertain. Yet, for centuries, the Rarámuri have managed and harvested the Sierra and barrancas in a sustainable manner. Pockets of small fields grow in the bottomlands and arroyos of the Sierra, while milpas and terraces, some at 45-degree angles, pose in bright-green contrast to the oak forests along the upper reaches of the barrancas. Making optimum use of arable land is a skill developed from centuries of a relationship to the Sierra and from a philosophy of *iwígara* borne from the place.

Rarámuri land management and resource use are harmonized with ecological ethics that positively affect their local environments. The Rarámuri understand that cultural survival is directly linked to biological survival of one's homeland. Over the centuries, methods of land use were developed that adhered to this understanding. Horticultural and agricultural techniques included selective coppicing, pruning, harvesting, gathering, incipient management, cultivation, transplanting, vegetative propagation, sowing, discriminate burning, and weeding.

Rarámuri agroecology and agroforestry have long sustained the culture as well as the ecosystem with which they live. Gathering techniques, such as that of collection of basket materials, have enhanced the functioning of ecosystems for centuries. These actions have influenced the diversity of species at a morphophysiological, ecological, and even evolutionary level. Through intentional and sometimes accidental plant dispersal, alteration of the forest with controlled burning, and selective pruning and coppicing, the Rarámuri have contributed to the quality and functioning of their environments. Their practices affected the reproduction of plant populations by modifying genetic compositions and species interactions. This is logical and easy to comprehend when it's understood that Rarámuri cultural priorities are also ecological and, therefore, hold the world together for the people as well as the animals and plants.

Psychological manifestations of this kincentric ecology are more difficult to document. Through conversations and careful observation, however, it is possible. An older Rarámuri teacher, Lencho, prefers to collect some of his medicinal plants from a particular *rincón*, or corner, of a large arroyo. He collects from other favorite locations as well, all of which, he says, "are places where the best plants grow." Walking to his *rincón* one day, we passed several plants of the same species we were intending to harvest. When questioned as to why we did not collect those plants, Lencho asserted, "Those plants are not right to collect because they are in the wrong place." Later, after I had had time to survey the path that we quickly walked along on the way to Lencho's *rincón*, I was able to stop and study the little colonies of plants. I realized the populations of plants that we passed there were low when compared to those that were eventually harvested.

There is an understanding that harvesting threatened populations is not ecologically sound. Yet Lencho would not explain the situation in this manner. He suggests that the *iwígara* in these low population areas is *ta umeruame*, or "weak," and must therefore be allowed to strengthen before the plants there are of any use. Later, he explained to me that collecting the plants in the *rincón* was good because thinning them out actually helps the *iwígara* in the other plants to strengthen. He mentioned, "Their roots become entangled which weakens their breath." In addition, he said, "the plants like to be near each other since they share their breaths." Experience, worldview, and understanding told him which populations were harvestable.

Wild edible plants are treated with the same respect as the medicinals. When collecting wild onions called *sibo* (*Allium longifolium*), the Rarámuri often select the larger bulbs, leaving the smaller ones in the ground to promote a second harvest. In addition, the Rarámuri use digging sticks to harvest the bulbs. As a result, the ground in which the onions grow is continuously disturbed. Not surprisingly, there are numerous ecological articles demonstrating how the disturbance in some habitats actually encourages plant diversity and further growth of some plants. A symbiotic relationship then exists between the Rarámuri and the onions. Disturbance of the sod and selective harvesting encourage the populations and ensure a harvest of onions.

Jesusita, Lencho, and other Rarámuri represent a tradition of conservation that relies on a reciprocal relationship with nature whereby the idea of *iwígara* becomes an affirmation of caretaking responsibilities and an assurance of sustainable subsistence and harvesting. It is a realization that the Sierra Madres is a place of nurturing that is full of relatives with whom all breath is shared. Their practices are an expression of Rarámuri traditional ecological knowledge and represent the practical knowledge that has been generated over centuries of living on the Spine of the Earth, the Sierra Madres of Chihuahua, Mexico. This knowledge is a reflection of a way of being or what may be considered a way of life. This is not so much a lifestyle, which often suggests choice, but just being. It is not a movement that can be joined, but rather a resilient worldview from which the people draw whole thinking approaches to every action and choice related to people and place.

When individuals in our modern society support a movement, an idea, or the mission of a nonprofit attempting to restore or preserve wild lands, those people are choosing to symbolically affiliate with that group. For the most part, we do this with our money, which, in essence, is a symbol that reflects our Western worldview. Some of us have more symbols than others, but the important concept is that we all share and support the use of a symbol and affiliate our identities and sense of self to it. Affiliation with a group is a result of human DNA. Connection to a group means better chances of survival. Today, we are not trying to survive on the African savanna, but look to the protection of wild lands, traditional foodways, whales, and rain forests as key to the survival of the species. Whales, hardwood trees, and landscapes are "real" things. They can be visited, touched, and even eaten if so desired. When something is tactile, it activates that portion of our brain that is constantly working to help us make sense of the chaos running around in our immediate environments. A live animal or a tree, when sensed, gets added to our domain of "real" things from which we can draw when trying to categorize the growing data being tossed at us. Tactile-ness is essential to human cognition because so much of our communication strategies are based on abstract metaphors that draw from concrete images. When a large environmental or conservation group suggests that it hopes we will contribute to its struggle so that it can purchase a piece of rangeland that we have never actually seen, we are apt to support it because we can envision grass and the animals that might live on it. The vision is drawn from our experiences. The abstract notion of supporting something gets blended with the concrete understanding of grassland. The mental blend then transforms into a new mental understanding that we can relate to on a "real" level, which leads us to pull out our checkbook. It becomes something that we can affiliate with. This is why support for an idea is much more difficult to gather from individuals. The key is to cultivate a way to demonstrate how the idea can become something that people can affiliate with in a tactile manner. In other words, how can resilience, whole thinking, and eating the landscape be poured into a mug? The future of our foods, our lands, our economies, and everything that we come into contact with depends on our ability to reconfigure this notion of a whole enchilada.

Further Reading

The information for this writing has resulted largely from my years of drinking coffee, eating ancestral foods, and just being with the people mentioned in the book. Still, some of the ideas and data have been derived from various other writers, academics, and thinkers. Here is a chapter-by-chapter list of readings that one may search through for additional information.

Chapter 1. In My Grandmother's Kitchen

Shiva, Vandana, *Biopiracy: The Plunder of Nature and Knowledge*. Cambridge, MA: South End Press, 1999.

Silko, Leslie Marmon, *Yellow Woman and a Beauty of the Spirit*. New York: Simon & Schuster, 1997.

Chapter 2. Sharing Breath

Fayhee, John, "Beating Feet and Pounding Brews With the Tarahumaras," *Rocky Mountain Sports & Fitness Magazine*, Sept.(1987)pp. 12-13.

Fontana, Bernard L., & John P. Schaefer, *Tarahumara: Where Night Is the Day of the Moon*. Tucson: University of Arizona Press, 1997.

Lumholtz, Carl, *Unknown Mexico, Volumes 1 & 2—A Record of Five Years' Exploration Among the Tribes of the Western Sierra Madre; In the Tierra Caliente of Tepic and Jalisco; and Among the Tarascos of Michoacan*. New York Qontro Classic Books, 2010.

Pennington, Campbell, *The Tarahumara of Mexico: Their Environment and Material Culture*. Salt Lake City: University of Utah Press, 1963.

Salmón, Enrique, "Sharing Breath: Some Links Between Land, Plants, and People." In Alison Deming & Lauret Savoy, eds., *The Colors of Nature*. Minneapolis, MN: Milkweed Editions, 2002.

Salmón, Enrique, "Kincentric Ecology." In Jesse Ford & D. Martinez, eds., *Traditional Ecological Knowledge, Ecosystem Science, and Environmental*

Management. Ecological Applications (Invited Feature Issue) 10, no. 5 (October 2000).

Salmón, Enrique, "Tarahumara Healing Practices," *Shaman's Drum*, no. 24 (Summer 1991).

Chapter 3. Pojoaque Pueblo and a Garden of the Ancients

Ford, Richard I., ed., *Prehistoric Food Production in North America*. Anthropological Papers, No. 75. Ann Arbor: Museum of Anthropology, University of Michigan, 1985.

Gunderson, Lance, & C. S. Hollings, eds., *Panarchy: Understanding Transformations in Human and Natural Systems*. Washington, DC: Island Press, 2001.

Ortman, Scott G., "Conceptual Metaphor in the Archaeological Record: Methods and an Example From the American Southwest." *American Antiquity* 65, no. 4 (2000): 613–45.

Varien, Mark D., *Sedentism and Mobility in a Social Landscape: Mesa Verde and Beyond*. Tucson: University of Arizona Press, 1999.

Vivian, R. Gwinn, *Chacoan Prehistory of the San Juan Basin*. New York: Academic Press, 1990.

Chapter 4. We Still Need Rain Spirits

Lekson, Stephan H., ed., *The Archeology of Chaco Canyon: An Eleventh-Century Pueblo Regional Center*. Sante Fe, NM: SAR Press, 2006.

Nazarea, Virginia, *Cultural Memory and Biodiversity*. Tucson: University of Arizona Press, 2006.

Whiting, Alfred A., *Ethnobotany of the Hopi*. New York: AMS Press, 1978.

Chapter 5. Bounty among the Saguaro

Abram, David, *The Spell of the Sensuous: Perception and Language in a More-Than-Human World*. New York: Vintage, 1997.

Cabeza de Vaca, Alvar Nunez, *The Account: Alvar Nunez Cabeza de Vaca's Relacion*. Houston, TX: Arte Publico Press, 1993.

Evers, Larry, & Felipe Molina, *Yaqui Deer Songs: Maso Bwikam*. Tucson: University of Arizona Press, 1987.

Judge, James W., "Chaco Canyon–San Juan Basin." In Linda S. Cordell & George J. Gunnerman, eds., *Dynamics of Southwest Prehistory*. Washington, DC: Smithsonian Institution Press, 1989.

Kozak, David L., *Surrendering to Diabetes: An Embodied Response to Perceptions of Diabetes and Death in the Gila River Indian Community.* Omega 35:347-359. 1997.

Malinowski, Bronislaw, *Magic, Science and Religion and Other Essays.* Boston: Beacon Press, 1948.

Rosch, Eleanor, C. Mervis, W. Gray, D. Johnson, and P. Boyes-Braem. 1976, "Basic objects in natural categories." Cognitive Psychology 8:392-439.

Salmón, Enrique, "Traditional Diet and Health in Northwest Mexico." In Gregory Cajete, ed., *A People's Ecology: Explorations in Sustainable Living.* Santa Fe, NM: Clear Light Publishers, 1999.

Varela, Francisco, Evan F. Thompson, & Eleanor Rosch, *The Embodied Mind.* Cambridge, MA: MIT Press, 1991.

Whorf, Benjamin, *Language, Thought, and Reality,* ed. John Carroll. Cambridge, MA: MIT Press, 1956.

Chapter 6. Small Fields for Large Impacts on the Colorado Plateau

Abbey, Edward, *Desert Solitaire.* Old Tappan, NJ: Touchstone, 1990.

Nabhan, Gary P., & Stephen Trimble, *The Geography of Childhood.* Boston: Beacon Press, 1995.

Pattie, James Ohio, *The Personal Narrative of James O. Pattie: The True Wild West of New Mexico and California.* Torrington, WY: Narrative Press, 2001.

Powell, John Wesley, *The Exploration of the Colorado River and Its Canyons.* New York: Penguin Classics, 2003.

Chapter 7. Highways of Diversity and Querencia in Northern New Mexico

Alonso De Herrera, Gabriel, *Ancient Agriculture: Roots and Application of Sustainable Farming,* with an Introduction by Juan Estevan Arellano. Layton, UT: Gibbs Smith, 2006.

Chapter 8. Singing to Turtles, Singing for Divine Fire

Felger, Richard S., *People of the Desert and Sea: Ethnobotany of the Seri Indians.* Tucson: University of Arizona Press, 1992.

Momaday, N. S., *In the Presence of the Sun: Stories and Poems, 1961–1991.* Albuquerque: University of New Mexico Press, 2009.

Nabhan, Gary P., *Singing the Turtles to Sea: The Comcáac (Seri) Art and Science of Reptiles.* Berkeley: University of California Press, 2003.

Scott, Clay, *Mapping Our Places—Voices from the Indigenous Communities Mapping Initiative.* Berkley, CA, 2006.

Chapter 9. A New American Indian Cuisine

Frank, Lois Ellen, *Foods of the Southwest Indian Nations.* Berkeley, CA: Ten Speed Press, 2002.

Nelson, Melissa K., *Original Instructions: Indigenous Teachings for a Sustainable Future.* Rochester, VT: Bear & Company, 2008.

Petrini, Carlo, ed., *Slow Food: Collected Thoughts on Taste, Tradition, and the Honest Pleasures of Food.* White River Junction, VT: Chelsea Green, 2001.

Chapter 10. The Whole Enchilada

Forbes, Peter, *The Great Remembering: Further Thoughts on Land, Soul and Society.* White River Junction, VT: Trust for Public Land/Chelsea Green, 2001.

Index

About the Author

Enrique Salmón is head of the American Indian Studies Program at Cal State University, East Bay located in Hayward, California. He has a BS from Western New Mexico University, an MAT in Southwestern Studies from Colorado College, and a PhD in Anthropology from Arizona State University. Enrique has been a Scholar in Residence at the Heard Museum and a program officer for the Greater Southwest and Northern Mexico regions for The Christensen Fund. Enrique has published several articles and chapters on indigenous ethnobotany, agriculture, nutrition, and traditional ecological knowledge. He also has been invited to speak at numerous conferences and symposia on the topics of cultivating resilience, indigenous solutions to climate change, ethnobiology of Native North America, ethnobotany of the Greater Southwest, poisonous plants that heal, bioculturally diverse regions as refuges of hope and resilience, and the language and library of indigenous ecological knowledge.